The KIDS' Pocket Calculator Game Book

BOOKS BY THE AUTHORS

Edwin Schlossberg:
Wordswordswords
Projex (Coauthor)
Einstein and Beckett

John Brockman:
(AS EDITOR)
Real Time 1
Real Time 2
About Bateson: Essays on Gregory Bateson
(AS AUTHOR)
By the Late John Brockman
37
Afterwords

Edwin Schlossberg and John Brockman (Coauthors):
The Pocket Calculator Game Book
The Philosopher's Game
The Pocket Calculator Game Book #2
The Kids' Pocket Calculator Game Book

The KIDS' Pocket Calculator Game Book

By EDWIN SCHLOSSBERG
and JOHN BROCKMAN

WILLIAM MORROW AND COMPANY, INC.
New York   1977

Printed in the United States of America.

1 2 3 4 5 6 7 8 9 10

Library of Congress Cataloging in Publication Data

Schlossberg, Edwin.
The kids' pocket calculator game book.
SUMMARY: Each chapter explains a specific mathematical principle and then teaches it through a puzzle and games using a pocket calculator.
1. Calculating-machines—Problems, exercises, etc.—Juvenile literature. 2. Mathematical recreations—Problems, exercises, etc.—Juvenile literature. [1. Calculating machines—Problems, exercises, etc. 2. Mathematical recreations—Problems, exercises, etc.]
I. Brockman, John (date), joint author. II. Title.
QA75.S337   513'.028'5   77-23933
ISBN 0-688-03233-8   ISBN 0-688-08233-5 pbk.

Designed by SALLIE BALDWIN

Contents

The
KIDS'
Pocket
Calculator
Game Book

Introduction

The Kids' Pocket Calculator Game Book will give you a chance to have some fun with your pocket calculator. And while you're having fun, playing games with your friends, solving puzzles by yourself, you just might learn some math. Painlessly. The easy way.

Mathematics is a language we learn in order to talk about things with the least possible confusion. The rules of math are no more difficult than those of everyday language. We learn to talk through the activity of listening and talking. Math can be learned in much the same way. While we can never replace serious classroom study, we believe that by playing the puzzles and games in this book, you can learn a great deal about the fundamentals of math, information that will help you in the classroom. The puzzles and games in the book will give you an opportunity to experiment, to make mistakes, and to have competitive and cooperative excitement and fun.

This book begins with some of the most basic rules and ideas of math and progresses to some of the more complex ideas. You can begin anywhere in the book if you want, but we suggest proceeding through the investigation of ideas as we have presented them ... from beginning to end.

There are twenty chapters. Each is designed around a central concept. First, you play the one-person puzzle and learn the basic ideas of the chapter. Second, you share these ideas with someone else in the two-person game, and then you gather a group of three or more players for a group game.

Your pocket calculator is constructed with many of the most fundamental ideas and rules of math already automatically integrated into its circuitry. But how do you know your calculator is operating correctly? You don't... unless you know the fundamentals of math behind its operation. Several things can go wrong with your calculator. Sometimes the calculator will have imperfections which cause them to give wrong answers. Other times, the batteries run down. Often when calculators have been bounced around they come up with strange results.

The pocket calculator is a useful tool. It allows you to carry out quickly operations that would take much longer on paper. It also suggests things that can be done with it. But the key thing to remember is that just like any tool, it is not useful without a good operator.

The games in this book have been created to assist you in being a good operator and to suggest many uses for your pocket calculator. You can think of each of the puzzles and games as a starting point, a place from which you can develop, change, and improve, once you understand more about how your calculator works, about the language of math, and about the nature of these games.

Each manufacturer develops its own integrated circuit, on which is printed the logic that operates your calculator. The rules and instructions of these puzzles and games are based on the way most calculators function. But your calculator might have a different logic. To see if this is the case, read the first chapter and play the puzzle and games. If you run into problems, read the instruction manual that came with your calculator and then adapt the rules of operation of your particular calculator. Most calculators will work fine. So, don't worry.

In writing the puzzles and games, we assumed some understanding about words and use of the pocket calculator. The following list of rules and terms will help supply you with the basics and get you into playing the puzzles and games.

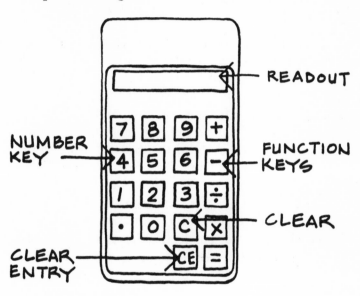

DIGITS AND NUMBERS

Digits are like letters, and numbers are like words. Words are made of letters, and numbers are made of digits. For example: the number 632 is made up of the digits 6 and 3 and 2. 632 is a three-digit number.

OPERATIONS

These are + (add), − (subtract), × (multiply), ÷ (divide). An operation is what you do with one number to another number. You add one number to another number, you subtract one number from another number, you multiply one number by another number, you divide one number by another number. The operations refer to adding, subtracting, multiplying, or dividing.

PLUS AND MINUS NUMBERS

A plus number is a number greater than 0 (for example: 6 is a plus number). A minus number is a number less than 0 (for example: −6 is a minus number).

DECIMAL POINTS AND DECIMAL NUMBERS

A decimal point is the point separating a whole number from a part less than 1. For example: If you have ten and a half apples, you will see 10.5 on the calculator. Then .5 is the same as ½ and is a decimal number. The decimal part of a number is less than 1. The numbers to the right of the decimal point on the calculator are decimal numbers (for example: .5 in 10.5).

A fraction such as ½ is shown on the calculator as .5, since it is $\frac{5}{10}$ or half of 1. Thus, when a fraction comes up in a game or puzzle, it is the same as a decimal number (a part of 1 such as ½ or ¼, which is shown on the calculator as .5 or .25).

SOME OTHER POINTS TO REMEMBER

Zero is always considered a digit unless the rules state otherwise.

The Lead Digit of a number is the digit farthest to the left. In the number 76895, 7 is the Lead Digit.

In some games, the instructions ask you to eliminate a digit from a number, often the Lead Digit. To do this, you must subtract the value of the digit. For example: To eliminate the Lead Digit 9 from 98765, you must subtract 90000, not just 9: 98765 − 90000 = 8765.

A Decimal Number is a number which has both whole and decimal numbers. 354.98 is a Decimal Number in which 354 is the whole number, and .98 the decimal part. A Decimal Number is even if the last digit to the right in the decimal part of the number is even. For example: 34.568 is even, but 34.567 is odd.

In some games it will be necessary to subtract a *larger* number from a *smaller* number. The easiest way to do this is to subtract the larger number from the smaller number and then multiply the result by −1. For example: You have 678 in your calculator and must subtract it from 987. In order to avoid taking 678 out of the calculator ("clearing" the calculator), entering 987 and then subtracting 678, you can subtract 987 from 678 (678 − 987 = −309) and then multiply the result by −1 (−309 × −1 = 309). This is a handy and faster way of doing it.

However, some calculators do not handle minus numbers properly and cannot carry out this operation correctly. To test your calculator to see if it does handle minus numbers properly, subtract −1 from −1: −1 − (−1) = 0. If you get −2, then you will have to *add* when you see two minus signs in a row. You would change −1 − (−1) to −1 + 1 = 0. And, in the case of subtracting as above, you would do the following: 678 − 987 = −309, and then clear the calculator and reenter 309. If your calculator has a −/+ key, this key shifts the number on the display from minus to plus or plus to minus, and enables you to make the change very easily: 678 − 987 = − 309; then press the −/+ key and the result is 309.

In some of the games there are numbers and operations written in a series. For example: 3 × 5 + 9 − 2 and so on. It is important that you do the operation BE-TWEEN two numbers before you proceed to the next operation and next number. For example, in the above series of numbers and operations you must multiply 3 × 5 before adding 9. If you go out of order you will get the wrong answer. In some cases you can put parentheses around two numbers and an operation. For example, 4 + (3 × 5). In this case, and only when there are parentheses, you would multiply 3 × 5 FIRST and then add the result to 4.

Many calculators have only 6 places in the readout. When you divide one number by another and the result is not rational (this is explained in the Ratios Chapter) the result often extends beyond the 6 places of the readout. For example 10 ÷ 3 = 3.3333333333333. The calculator then ROUNDS OFF the number to 6 places. If the seventh digit is less than 5 then the calculator ROUNDS DOWN so that the number would read 3.33332. If the number were 5.6666666 then the calculator would ROUND UP to 5.66667. Your calculator might operate differently. Try a few experiments to see how your calculator ROUNDS OFF because in some games you may find that the rounding off will make a slight difference in the result you get.

You should calculate all the possibilities before making a play. The pocket calculator, because of its speed, should be used to calculate your best move.

The Kids' Pocket Calculator Game Book is the third in a series by Edwin Schlossberg and John Brockman. Once you have played your way through this book, we suggest that you extend the range and types of games you can play by using *The Pocket Calculator Game Book* and *The Pocket Calculator Game Book #2*.

Edwin Schlossberg invented the puzzles and games and drafted the book, which was developed and edited by John Brockman. Lyn Horton assisted in preparation of the manuscript. The cartoons are by Alex Tiani, the art work by Vincent Trocchia. Katinka Matson contributed to the final editing. James Landis and Jack Looney, our editors, have given valuable assistance in all stages of the development of the book.

EDWIN SCHLOSSBERG   JOHN BROCKMAN
Chester, Massachusetts   *New York City*

CHAPTER ONE:
Counting on Counting

Your calculator can add, subtract, multiply, and divide very quickly. But how do you know that your calculator is correct? To be able to know if your calculator is correct, you have to be able to add, subtract, multiply, and divide as well as the calculator so that when the answers appear on the calculator readout, you know if they are right. You have to be able to count on yourself. A weak battery, an imperfection in the circuitry, an accidental drop, and your calculator may give just slightly wrong answers, or no answers at all.

To discover your own abilities to count, your ability to count on yourself, take two trips through the COUNTING MAZE below, first without the calculator, then with your calculator.

THE COUNTING MAZE

FINISH / START

112 / 6×7	86 / 29×3	54 / 53-26	40 / 77-6	43 / 118÷2	7 / 82÷41	50 / 6×5	79 / 29×2	87 / 19×2	29 / 37×2	71 / 25×3	76 / 13×7
84 / 9+8	108 / 53×2	14 / 8×4	74 / 92÷2	95 / 178÷2	13 / 50-4	31 / 87÷3	57 / 72÷4	78 / 13×5	81 / 11×6	51 / 41×2	89 / 10×10
10 / 11×2	85 / 43×2	30 / 5×5	2 / 86-33	48 / 13×3	77 / 7×1	24 / 7×3	72 / 19×4	17 / 4×10	100 / 132-53	88 / 6×8	97 / 17×6
47 / 91-30	49 / 4×11	34 / 7×14	18 / 45÷9	42 / 8÷2	70 / 49÷7	80 / 100÷10	16 / 99÷9	75 / 7×11	45 / 6×16	99 / 7×5	19 / 4×4
98 / 23×3	21 / 9+4	39 / 60÷10	52 / 17×5	32 / 8×10	11 / 17×2	66 / 5×4	23 / 96÷4	67 / 62÷2	38 / 97-24	91 / 19×3	1 / 129-12
6 / 7×4	61 / 47×2	27 / 31×2	36 / 44-7	22 / 14×5	64 / 7×9	62 / 8×11	90 / 31×3	4 / 27÷9	65 / 6×18	105 / 102÷2	56 / 8×8
106 / 13×8	12 / 9+6	53 / 13×2	3 / 9×9	46 / 18×4	5 / 9×6	15 / 12-3	8 / 7×2	41 / 59-16	55 / 9×11	93 / 29-10	35 / 6×6
59 / 23×4	69 / 94-42	44 / 9×5	82 / 125-42	33 / 96÷12	68 / 97-30	20 / 10×6	58 / 21×5	96 / 46÷2	73 / 17×4	110 / 7×16	102 / 47÷47
25 / 7×12	28 / 40-7	94 / 19×5	63 / 5+7	104 / 123÷3	26 / 9×10	37 / 5×10	92 / 143-46	9 / 11×5	83 / 13×6	60 / 8×7	107 / 10×11

THE COUNTING MAZE

Start in the box in the upper lefthand corner with the numbers at the bottom of the box, 6 × 7. Then find the box that has the answer to 6 × 7 at the top of the box. Continue by doing the operation in the bottom of that box (the answer to 6 × 7 is 42, and the operation at the bottom is 8 ÷ 2). Now find the box that has the answer to 8 ÷ 2 at the top, and so on, until you arrive back at the box with 112 at the top.

It will take some time to do the counting maze so don't expect to finish in a hurry.

QUICK COUNT

2 Players
2 Calculators
Blackboard or Large Sheet of Paper
Chalk or Pencils

OBJECT OF THE GAME

To be the fastest and most accurate calculator.

THE PLAY

One player writes a series of numbers and operations on the blackboard or on a large sheet of paper which can be seen by both players from a distance of six feet. For example: $6 + 9 \times 4 - 3 + 89 \times 56 + 123 - 78 \div 2 + 10$. The player *does not* write what this series of operations equals.

The two players stand six feet apart facing each other with their turned-off calculators in their hands and their hands at their sides. One of the players says, "Calculate!" Both players turn on their calculators and perform the series of numbers and operations written on the board as fast as possible. To win, a player must finish first *and* have the correct answer. Check your answers after each round to make sure they are correct. If the player who finishes first has the wrong answer, no one wins.

In the second round, the player who did not write the first series of numbers and operations writes a new series.

Make the series of numbers and operations more difficult with each round.

Play the game at least five times. The player who wins the most rounds wins the shoot-out.

SAMPLE PLAY

Player A writes on blackboard: $8 \div 4 + 52 \div 9 \times 20 - 18$

One of the players says, "Calculate!"

A calculates 102	B calculates 121.999 and finishes first
B checks A's answer	A checks B's answer
A is right.	B is wrong. No winner.

Player B writes on blackboard: $20 \times 5 - 11 \div 20 \times 15 + 129 - 49$

One of the players says, " Calculate!'

A calculates 146.75	B calculates 146.75 and finishes first
B checks A's answer	A checks B's answer
A is right.	B is right, and wins round.

Player A writes on blackboard: $153 \times 18 \div 9 + 400 - 86 \times 2 \div 8$

One of the players says, "Calculate!"

A calculates 177.14285 and finishes first	B calculates 155
B checks A's answer	A checks B's answer
A is wrong.	B is wrong. No winner.

---

15 SECONDS

4 or More Players
1 Calculator
Blackboard and Chalk or
Large Sheet of Paper and Pencil
Watch

OBJECT OF THE GAME

For the players to cooperate in skilled, fast, and accurate operations.

THE PLAY

The players choose an Operator. The Operator chooses a series of numbers (one- or two-digit numbers) and operations ($+$, $-$, $\times$, $\div$) that has three numbers and three operations per player, including the Operator. However, the Operator puts three numbers and three operations at the end of the series and his/her last operation is ALWAYS $=$. For example: If there were four players, then the Operator would write twelve numbers (one- or two-digit) and twelve operations with the last operation being $=$. This series of numbers is written on a large sheet of paper or on a blackboard so that all the players can see it. Once the series is written the Operator does the calculations and writes the answer on a piece of paper, which is not shown to the other players.

The players sit in a circle or in a row. The Operator says, "Calculate" and passes the calculator to the first player in the row or circle. That player does the first three numbers and operations and then passes it to the next player, who does the next three numbers and operations and so on until the calculator is passed back to the Operator who does the last three numbers, two operations, and then presses the = sign.

The Operator has a watch and times each player. Each player has only 15 seconds to complete the operations. If a player fails to complete the operations in 15 seconds, the next player must do the ones not done PLUS his/her own.

Once all the numbers and operations are done, the Operator checks the answer on the calculator with the original answer that was written down. If it is the same, the group is doing well.

A new Operator is chosen for the next round. The numbers and the series of operations should become more complicated to add fun to the game. The game should be played until everyone has had a turn being the Operator.

SAMPLE PLAY

A is Operator and writes on the blackboard:

$8 \times 3 + 12 - 1 + 63 + 10 + 6 \times 12 + 2 \div 4 - 5 \times 12 = 4050$

A then calculates the answer = 4050 and writes it on a piece of paper.

A says, "Calculate!" and passes the calculator to B.

B calculates $8 \times 3 + 12 -$ and passes it to C.

C calculates $1 + 63 + 10 +$ and passes it to D.

D calculates $6 \times 12 + 2 \div$ and passes it to A (the Operator).

A calculates $4 - 5 \times 12 =$ and looks at the answer, which is 4040.

A then checks it against the written answer, which was 4050.

The group was not perfect but was almost right.
Player B becomes the Operator, and the game continues.

CHAPTER TWO:
How Many Numbers Are There?

How many numbers are there? When you count how many numbers there are, you have used numbers to count them. You used numbers to count the number of numbers. To count the most numbers you can, you must use numbers to count them. Press the 9 button on your calculator until all the places on the readout show 9's. Is this the largest number that your calculator can count?

If you think so, then subtract that number of 9's from those you already entered in the calculator. Now, subtract that number of 9's again. You can think of starting the number of numbers you can count from minus 99999999 as well as from 0.

The answer to the question, "How many numbers are there?" is "All the numbers that you can count." Your pocket calculator can display many numbers. Some calculators have the ability to display the number on the readout times 10 with 99 zeros after it. If written out this would be 999999000000000000000000 0000000000000000000000000000000000000000000000000 000000000000000000000000000000000. And then you could display the minus numbers too!

OVERSHOOT PUZZLE

Now that you are familiar with the numbers in your calculator, try the following puzzle. Which of the following numbers will be larger than the readout of your calculator?

SAMPLE PLAY

$1 \times 2 = ?$
$1 \times 2 \times 3 = ?$
$1 \times 2 \times 3 \times 4 = ?$
$1 \times 2 \times 3 \times 4 \times 5 = ?$
$1 \times 2 \times 3 \times 4 \times 5 \times 6 = ?$
$1 \times 2 \times 3 \times 4 \times 5 \times 6 \times 7 = ?$
$1 \times 2 \times 3 \times 4 \times 5 \times 6 \times 7 \times 8 = ?$
$1 \times 2 \times 3 \times 4 \times 5 \times 6 \times 7 \times 8 \times 9 = ?$
$1 \times 2 \times 3 \times 4 \times 5 \times 6 \times 7 \times 8 \times 9 \times 10 = ?$
$1 \times 2 \times 3 \times 4 \times 5 \times 6 \times 7 \times 8 \times 9 \times 10 \times 11 = ?$
$1 \times 2 \times 3 \times 4 \times 5 \times 6 \times 7 \times 8 \times 9 \times 10 \times 11 \times 12 = ?$

Guess which one will go over and then multiply them. If you have a six-digit readout, you should get to the eighth line. If you have an eight-digit readout, you should get all but one. If you have a ten-digit readout, you should be able to multiply them all.

If you do have a ten-digit readout, try to guess how high you can go after twelve before you go over your readout. If you go over, you lose.

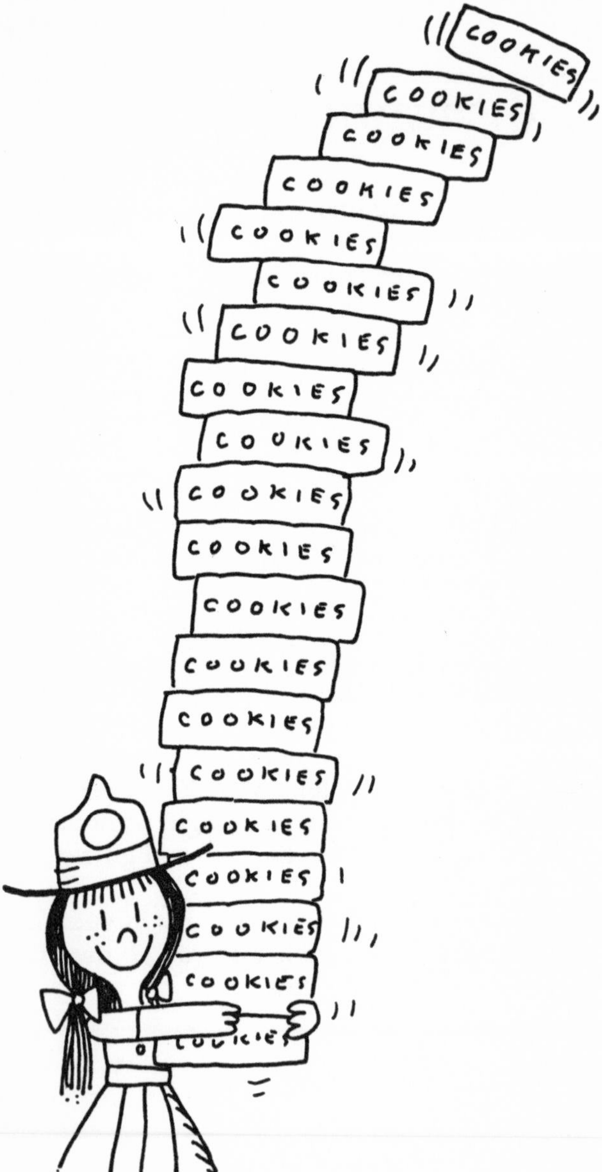

WATCHOUT

2 Players
2 Calculators (with identical number of digits in the display)

OBJECT OF THE GAME
To increase your number without going over the capability of your calculator.

THE PLAY
Each player enters a three-digit number in his/her calculator, no digit the same, and zero cannot be the first digit (for example: 012 may not be used). Player A then says a one-digit number (between 1 and 9). Both players multiply by this number. Then Player B says a one-digit number and both players multiply.

Each player is trying to make the other player go over the limit of his/her calculator first. Each player has one chance during the game to PASS. BUT ONLY ONE CHANCE. If a player decides to pass, he or she says, "I pass."

At any time during the game, a player may say a two-digit number and multiply if the player thinks that it will be safe for him or her and will push the other player over the limit.

If both players go over the limit, no one wins and the game starts again. Play three games to see who is the winner.

Note: Players may not use minus numbers such as −987. And, players must use new three-digit starting numbers for each game.

SAMPLE PLAY
(Both players have six-digit display calculators)

Player A enters 123	Player B enters 102
Player A says, "Multiply by 9"	
123 × 9 = 1107	102 × 9 = 918
	Player B says, "10"
1107 × 10 = 11070	918 × 10 = 9180
Player A says, "5"	
11070 × 5 = 55350	9180 × 5 = 45900
	Player B says, "20"
Player A passes	
55350	45900 × 20 = 918000
Player A says, "2"	Player B passes
55350 × 2 = 110700	918000
	Player B says, "1"
110700 × 1 = 110700	918000 × 1 = 918000
Player A says, "3"	
110700 × 3 = 332100	918000 × 3 = OVERSHOOT
Player A wins.	

THE PICKLE GAME

3 or More Players
1 Calculator per Player

OBJECT OF THE GAME

For each player to make up a question that involves huge numbers for the other players to answer.

THE PLAY

Each player thinks up a question about something that has a large number of things in it and tries to guess the answer. For example: "How many pickles have been used by McDonald's?" After all the players have done this, Player A asks his/her question. The other players try to answer it.

Since many calculators only have six-digit readouts, you may have to count in millions. That is, instead of entering 6,000,000, enter 6, remembering that 6 stands for 6 million. This way you will be able to use larger numbers than your calculator can handle.

Each player who comes up with an answer that is acceptable to Player A gets one point. Then Player B asks a question, and so on until each player has asked a total of three questions.

The player's question must have a well-known fact as its basis. For example: It is well known that McDonald's has sold 20 billion hamburgers. If a player asks a question and another player does not know the facts upon which it is based, the player must supply some of the facts. For example: If a player does not know how many hamburgers McDonald's has sold, he or she must be told.

When the players figure out the answer to the question, they must explain how they arrived at that answer. For example: A player's answer is that McDonald's sold 3,800,000,000,000 pickles because each hamburger has an average of 3 slices of pickle. But some people don't like pickles so probably that equals 1 billion less hamburgers sold with pickles, and that there are 15 slices of pickle to a pickle, so the total pickles are 19 billion × 3 = 57,000,000,000,000 ÷ 15 = 3,800,000,000,000 pickles!

Each player must think up three questions for the other players to try to answer. The player with the most points after everyone has asked three questions wins.

Suggestions for questions:
How many three-letter words are there?
How many toes are there in the world?
How many people are asleep right now?
How many leaves are there in the world?

CHAPTER THREE:
Plus and Minus,
More or Less

When you count with numbers, you begin with none, or zero, and go to 1, then 2, then 3, and so on. If you count back from a number, for example from 4, you count 4, then 3, then 2, then 1 and then zero. Then you have minus numbers that signify the absence of things, for example: -2 which means 2 things not there. What happens when you add a number like 15 to a minus number like -10? You count from 0 to 15, and then back from 15, 10 places:

$$\rightarrow \quad \rightarrow \quad \rightarrow \quad \rightarrow \quad \rightarrow \quad \rightarrow \rightarrow$$
$$0,\ 1,\ 2,\ 3,\ 4,\ 5,\ 6, 7,\ 8, 9,\ 10,\ 11,\ 12,\ 13,\ 14,\ 15$$
$$-10\ -9\text{-}8\ \text{-}7\ \text{-}6\ \text{-}5\ \text{-}4\ \text{-}3\ \text{-}2\ \text{-}1\ \ 0$$
$$\leftarrow \quad \leftarrow \quad \leftarrow \quad \leftarrow \quad \leftarrow \quad \leftarrow$$

By adding 15 and -10, you get to 5. This is the same as subtracting 10 from 15. If you do this on your calculator you press 15, press the minus key, press 10, and then the equal key. But you can also press 15, press the addition key, and then press -10, then the equal key, and get the same result.

If you multiply a *positive* number by a *minus* number, you get a *minus* number. If you multiply a *minus* number by a *minus* number, you get a *positive* number. Why? Because multiplying is simply shorthand for adding. 2×3 means $3 + 3$. When you add a positive number a minus number of times, you get a minus number. If you add a minus number a minus number of times, it is like subtracting from subtracting, which results in adding. For example, $10 \times 3 = 30$. What you are doing is adding $10 + 10 + 10 = 30$. -10×3 is adding -10 -10 $-10 = -30$ and -10×-3 is $(-10) - (-10) - (-10) = 30$.

Therefore:

$$\text{Plus} \times \text{Plus} = \text{Plus}$$
$$\text{Minus} \times \text{Plus} = \text{Minus}$$
$$\text{Minus} \times \text{Minus} = \text{Plus}$$

PLUS/MINUS MAZE

The idea of this maze is to get from Start to Finish, following the instructions in each box and using the numbers in the boxes to arrive at Finish with 0 in your calculator.

Note: Some calculators do not handle minus numbers properly. To see if your calculator does, subtract -1 from -1: $-1 - (-1) = 0$. If you get -2, then you will have to add when you see two minus signs in a row. So, you would transform $-1 - (-1)$ into $-1 + 1 = 0$.

PLUS/MINUS MAZE

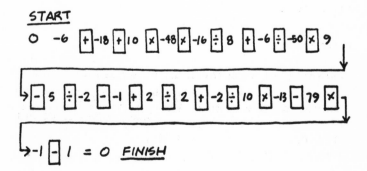

START

$0 \quad -6 \; [+]\,-18 \; [+]\,10 \; [\times]\,-48 \; [\times]\,-16 \; [\div]\,8 \; [+]\,-6 \; [\div]\,-50 \; [\times]\,9$

$\rightarrow [-]\,5 \; [\div]\,-2 \; [-]\,-1 \; [+]\,2 \; [\div]\,2 \; [+]\,-2 \; [\div]\,10 \; [\times]\,-13 \; [-]\,79 \; [\times]$

$\rightarrow -1 \; [-]\,1 = 0 \; \underline{FINISH}$

PLUS OR MINUS

2 Players
2 Calculators

OBJECT OF THE GAME

To have the largest number, plus or minus, after eight rounds.

THE PLAY

Each player enters a two-digit number in his/her calculator, no digits the same. Player A says an operation (+, −, ×, ÷), and Player B says another two-digit number (not the same as the one Player B entered). BUT, BEFORE PLAYERS ENTER THIS SECOND TWO-DIGIT NUMBER, Player A says either "plus" or "minus." If a player says "minus," then both players must use the second number they selected as a minus number. For example: If Player A had entered 25 and then enters ×, and then Player B had said 25, then Player A could say either "plus" or "minus." If Player A said "minus," then Player A would multiply 25 × −25 = −625. If Player A said "plus," then Player A would multiply 25 × 25 = 625.

Because each player is trying to get the largest number, plus or minus, each player must decide what is the best operation to say and whether it is better to say plus or minus.

Next, using the result of the previous round as the first number, Player B says an operation, and Player A says a two-digit number. Before the players enter this new two-digit number, Player B says "plus" or "minus."

The play continues for eight rounds. The player with the highest number wins. Remember, −878 will win over 877.

SAMPLE PLAY

A enters 12	B enters 27
A says, "Multiply"	B says, "50"
A says, "Minus"	
12 × −50 = −600	27 × −50 = −1350
	B says, "Multiply"
A says, "99"	B says, "Minus"
−600 × −99 = 59400	−1350 × −99 = 133650

A says, "Multiply"	B says, "10"
A says, "Minus"	
59400 × −10 = −594000	133650 × −10 = −1336500
	B says, "Divide"
A says, "11"	B says, "Minus"
−549000 ÷ −11 = 54000	−1336500 ÷ −11 = 121500

The game continues for eight rounds. The player with the highest number wins.

HI-LO

3 or More Players
1 Calculator per Player
Pencil and Paper

OBJECT OF THE GAME

To win the most out of ten rounds with the highest minus or plus number.

THE PLAY

Each player enters a two-digit number, plus or minus, in his or her calculator. Next, each player writes this number and its sign on a piece of paper and passes the paper to the player to the right. Again, each player writes the same number and its sign on the piece of paper passed to him, to the right of the first written number, and passes it on. The players continue to do this until the pieces of paper are back with their original owners.

Each player now uses this series of written numbers and tries to get the largest result possible, using the numbers in the order they are written. For example: A player's piece of paper reads: 10, −54, −34, 22. The player can use the numbers like this: $10 - (-54) - (-34) \times 22$. MULTIPLICATION MAY BE USED ONCE ONLY.

A player can try for a large minus number, since −878 will win over 877. The player with the largest result wins the round. Play continues for ten rounds; the player who wins the most rounds is the winner.

SAMPLE PLAY

| A enters −11 | B enters 14 | C enters 13 |
| A writes −11 | B writes 14 | C writes 13 |

They pass the paper around, each writing his or her own number and + or − sign on it to the right of the first number written. When all three have written their numbers three times, the papers are back with the original player.

| Player A has | Player B has | Player C has |
| −11, 14, 13 | 14, 13, −11 | 13, −11, 14 |

| Player A does | Player B does | Player C does |
| $-11 \times 14 + 13 = -141$ | $14 \times 13 - (-11) = 193$ | $13 \times -11 + 14 = -129$ |

Player B wins this round. (The players did not have to use multiplication first and then addition, but in this particular round they all did the operations in the same order. Players may do the operations in any order but they may not use multiplication more than once in a round.)

CHAPTER FOUR:
Even Odd and
Oddly Even

Even numbers can be divided by 2 without remainders. For example: $6 \div 2 = 3$, so 6 is an even number. But, $7 \div 2 = 3.5$, the .5 is leftover, so 7 is an odd number. When you multiply an even number by an even number, the result is an even number. When you multiply an even number by an odd number, the result is an even number. But, when you multiply an odd number by an odd number, the result is an odd number. Knowing this will allow you to predict what happens when you multiply, and also when you divide (dividing is the opposite of multiplying).

THE EVEN/ODD MAZE PUZZLE

To do the following puzzle, you must keep the readout on your calculator ODD for the first 10 steps, and then EVEN for the next 10 steps by choosing the operation ($+$, $-$, $\times$, $\div$) that will produce an ODD result in the first 10, and an EVEN result in the second 10. For example: If you have 5☐4 and you have to stay ODD, you must either add, $5 + 4 = 9$, or subtract, $5 - 4 = 1$, or divide, $5 \div 4 = 1.25$.

EVEN/ODD MAZE

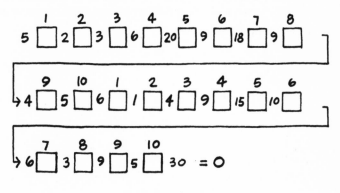

EVEN/ODD

2 Players
2 Calculators
Pencil and Paper

OBJECT OF THE GAME
To have the highest number for five rounds.

THE PLAY
The players decide who goes first. The first player is
the ODD player and can use the numbers 1,3,7,9. The
other player is the EVEN player and can use the numbers 2,4,6,8.

Each player enters one of his or her numbers into
his/her calculator. ODD says an operation (+, −, ×,
÷) and both players enter it and then enter another
one of their numbers. EACH PLAYER MAY USE HIS/
HER NUMBERS ONLY ONCE. Then both players

press the equal button. Now EVEN says an operation. MULTIPLICATION MAY BE SAID ONLY TWICE DURING THE FIVE ROUNDS OF THE GAME. Both players enter it, then enter another one of their numbers, and press the equal button. ODD says another operation, and EVEN says another operation and the round is over. The player with the highest number wins the round. The player winning five rounds wins the game.

SAMPLE PLAY

A decides to go first
so is ODD

can use 1, 3, 7, 9

enters 7

A says, "Multiply"
chooses $7 \times 9 = 63$

chooses $63 + 3 = 66$

A says, "Add"
chooses $66 + 1 = 67$

A wins the round and
has said, "Multiply," once

The game continues.

B is EVEN

can use 2, 4, 6, 8

enters 2

chooses $2 \times 8 = 16$

B says, "Add"
chooses $16 + 6 = 22$

chooses $22 + 4 = 26$

BIG MOUTH

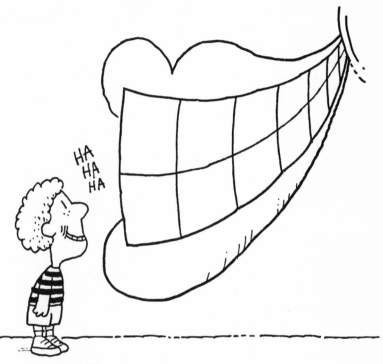

HA
HA
HA

4 or More Players
1 Calculator per Player
1 Coin

OBJECT OF THE GAME

For one team to get ten points.

THE PLAY

The players divide up into two teams. Each player now trades calculators with a member of the other team. Each player enters a three-digit number, no digits the same, into the traded calculator and passes it back to the owner. The players may NOT show their numbers to their other team members.

A player now flips a coin. If it turns up Heads, that player's team is ODD; the other team is EVEN. If it turns up Tails, that player's team is EVEN, and the other team is ODD. This means that each team *must stay EVEN or ODD* when the members combine their numbers.

One member of each team takes a turn being Big Mouth, the player who decides how to combine the numbers of his team *without having seen the numbers,* either by *multiplication* or *addition.* For example: Big Mouth says, "Add." The players show their numbers and then add them up. Or Big Mouth says, "Multiply," and the players combine their numbers through multiplication. For example: There are four players on each team. Player A has 345, B has 675, C has 874, and D has 216. If Big Mouth says, "Add," then the members add their numbers: $345 + 675 + 874 + 216 = 2110$, which is EVEN. If the team is supposed to be EVEN, they get one point. If the team is supposed to be ODD, they don't get a point. If both teams succeed in their assignment to be EVEN or ODD, then the team with the *highest* number gets one additional point. If neither team succeeds in its assignment of EVEN or ODD, then the team with the *lowest* total number gets one point.

Each round proceeds in the same manner, with players trading calculators and entering new numbers. The game continues until one team has ten points.

SAMPLE PLAY

	TEAM ONE		TEAM TWO	
	A	B	C	D
	passes calculator to C	passes calculator to D	passes calculator to A	passes calculator to B
	A enters 546	B enters 872	C enters 243	D enters 129
	passes calculator to C	passes calculator to D	passes calculator to A	passes calculator to B
After trade, calculators read:	243	129	546	872
	A flips coin; result is Tails so Team One is EVEN		and Team Two is ODD	
	A is Big Mouth		C is Big Mouth	
	A says, "Add"		C says, "Add"	
	243 + 129 = 372		546 + 872 = 1418	
	Stays EVEN		Does not stay ODD	
	Team One gets 1 point		Team Two gets 0 points	

A	B	C	D
passes calculator to C	passes calculator to D	passes calculator to A	passes calculator to B
A enters 456	B enters 137	C enters 983	D enters 146
passes calculator to C	passes calculator to D	passes calculator to A	passes calculator to B
After trade, calculators read:			
983	146	456	137
A flips coin; result is Tails so Team One is EVEN		and Team Two is ODD	
	B is Big Mouth		D is Big Mouth
	B says, "Multiply"		D says, "Add"
	$983 \times 146 = 143518$		$456 + 137 = 593$
	Stays EVEN		Stays ODD
Team One gets 1 point also gets 1 point for highest number		Team Two gets 1 point	
Total Score after two rounds:		Team Two has 1 point	
Team One has three points			

The game continues in this manner until one team has ten points and wins the game.

CHAPTER FIVE:
Zeroing In

Counting and using numbers are ways of representing objects. But what happens when there are no objects or when all the objects are gone? You say there are zero objects (0 objects). Five objects minus 5 objects equals 0 objects. Then zero is a number that counts THE ABSENCE OF OBJECTS! Also, zero is a number that is the evidence that things have been eliminated. You would not need it if there had been no things before you started to count.

When we write 0, we are really writing the result of an operation like $5 - 5$: $5 - 5 = 0$. When you use 0 in doing number operations you have to remember this. For example: When you multiply times 0 you are multiplying a number times the absence of numbers and so the result is the absence of numbers ($5 \times 0 = 0$). When you divide by 0 you are trying to count the number of absences of number in a number which is uncountable. How many times would the absence of numbers fit into 5? An uncountable number of times. We use the INFINITY to represent this uncountable number.

The ZERO ROUTES PUZZLE below is a map of the land of ZERO. In between the arrows on the routes the total of the operations equals zero. For example, if you start at the entrance at $+ 6$ and go to 31 your calculator must read zero. Then you can choose to go around Zero Lake (the total of that route is zero) or follow the outer route (the total between the.arrows is also zero).

You can make an entire trip around Zero Land and have zero as the result of any part of the journey *between two arrows* on the map.

ZERO ROUTES PUZZLE

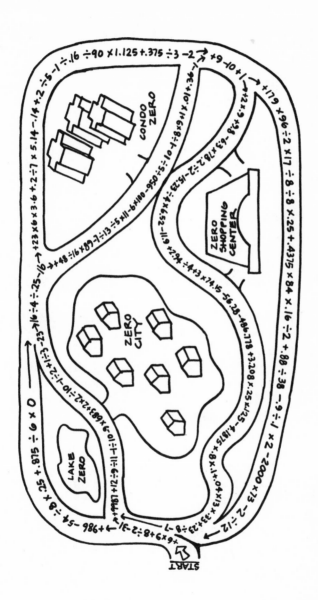

THE ZERO HERO

2 Players
2 Calculators
Pencil and Paper

OBJECT OF THE GAME

To have the calculator read zero at the end of the round and to win the most rounds, thus becoming the Zero Hero.

THE PLAY

Each player enters a three-digit number, no digits the same. Player A says an operation (+, −, ×, ÷) and then each of the players enters a number between 0 and 9. THE NUMBERS 0–9 MAY BE USED ONLY ONCE EACH DURING THE ROUND BY EACH PLAYER. The players do not tell each other what numbers they entered, but keep a record of it on a piece of paper.

Now Player B says an operation and the round continues until all the numbers have been used by each player. MULTIPLYING BY 0 MAY NOT BE USED AFTER THE FIFTH TURN OF THE ROUND. So, if a player wants to multiply by zero, the player must do it in the first 5 times that operations are said.

Since the object is to reduce the numbers to zero, players will use subtraction and division most often, but adding a number like 1 or 2 may make it easier to divide on the next turn. If a decimal number appears, the decimal MUST BE KEPT.

Remember that multiplying by 0 will result in 0. Because you can use the numbers 0–9 only once in a round, think ahead to what might happen in the future.

The player who has zero on his or her calculator is the winner. If both players fail to reach zero, then the player with the lowest absolute number wins the round. (The lowest absolute number means that 2 wins over −3 since the absolute value of −3 is 3.)

Play the game for ten rounds. The Zero Hero is the player who wins the most number of rounds.

SAMPLE PLAY

A enters 123

A says, "Add"
chooses 123 + 7 = 130

chooses 130 ÷ 5 = 26

A says, "Subtract"
chooses 26 − 6 = 20

chooses 20 × 4 = 80

A says, "Divide"
chooses 80 ÷ 8 = 10

chooses 10 − 9 = 1

A says, "Multiply"
chooses 1 × 2 = 2

chooses 2 + 1 = 3

A says, "Subtract"
chooses 3 − 3 = 0

chooses 0 + 0 = 0

A wins round.

B enters 654

chooses 654 + 6 = 660

B says, "Divide"
chooses 660 ÷ 4 = 165

chooses 165 − 9 = 156

B says, "Multiply"
chooses 156 × 0 = 0

chooses 0 ÷ 8 = 0

B says, "Subtract"
chooses 0 − 7 = −7

chooses −7 × 1 = −7

B says, "Add"
chooses −7 + 5 = −2

chooses −2 − 3 = −5

B says, "Add"
chooses −5 + 2 = −3

The play continues with the players entering new three-digit numbers for the next round.

CAPTAIN ZERO

3 or More Players
1 Calculator per Player

OBJECT OF THE GAME

To have either the most zeros or just zero after ten rounds of play.

THE PLAY

Each player enters a number from 1 to 10 in his or her calculator. The players choose who will be the first Captain Zero. (A new Captain Zero is chosen for each round.) Then each player presses an operation (+, −, ×, ÷), and Captain Zero gives one of the following four instructions:

A. Press 0 and then =
B. Press 10 and then =
C. Press 100 and then =
D. Press the number on your readout and then =.

All players, including Captain Zero, follow this instruction. For example: A player enters 4 and +. Captain Zero says, "Press 10 and =." So the player would have 4 + 10 = 14.

Another player becomes Captain Zero for the next round. Each player presses another operation with the following restrictions:

1. Multiplication can be used only 3 times
2. Addition can be used only 3 times
3. Subtraction can be used only 3 times
4. Division can be used only 2 times

so players must keep track of what operations they use. AND, Instruction A (Press 0 and =) CANNOT BE USED IN THE LAST ROUND.

A player who enters a number and multiplies and gets a result exceeding the capability of the calculator automatically loses the game. For example: A player has 10,000, and multiplied by 10,000 the result will probably exceed the capability of the calculator (calculator readout flashes or reads "error"). If the player is instructed to do this, the player must refuse and say, "Give me another instruction." If the player doesn't anticipate this happening, and follows the instruction, the player is out.

The player with 1 or more digits followed by 3 or more zeros wins over a player with 1 or more digits followed by 1 or 2 zeros. A player with 1 or more digits followed by 2 zeros wins over a player with 1 or more digits followed by zero. For example: 1000 wins over 3400; 300 wins over 1430, 10 wins over 34; 100 wins over 0. In the event of a tie in the number of zeros, the player with the highest number wins.

STRATEGY

Try to use the operations you select in such a way as to improve the chance of your having many zeros at the end of the game, or just zero. Many zeros is an easier goal than one zero (64000 is easier than 10).

SAMPLE PLAY

A	B	C
A enters 5	B enters 3	C enters 8
A is Captain Zero		
A presses $\times$	B presses $+$	C presses $-$
A says, "Instruction C"		
$5 \times 100 = 500$	$3 + 100 = 103$	$8 - 100 = -92$
A presses $+$	B is Captain Zero	
	B presses $\times$	C presses $+$
	B says, "Instruction C"	
$500 + 100 = 600$	$103 \times 100 = 10300$	$-92 + 100 = 8$
		C is Captain Zero
A presses $-$	B presses $+$	C presses $-$
		C says, "Instruction D"
$600 - 600 = 0$	$10300 + 10300 = 20600$	$8 - 8 = 0$
A is Captain Zero		
A presses $\times$	B presses $-$	C presses $\times$
A says, "Instruction A"		
$0 \times 0 = 0$	$20600 - 0 = 20600$	$0 \times 0 = 0$

A	B	C
	B is Captain Zero	
A presses ÷	B presses × B says, "Instruction C" $20600 \times 100 = 2060000$	C presses − $0 - 100 = -100$
$0 \div 100 = 0$		
		C is Captain Zero
A presses ÷	B presses + $2060000 + 2060000 =$ 4120000	C presses + C says, "Instruction D" $-100 + 100 = 0$
$0 \div 0 = 0$		
A is Captain Zero		
A presses − A says, "Instruction A" $0 - 0 = 0$	B presses − $4120000 - 0 = 4120000$	C presses ÷ $0 \div 0 = 0$
	B is Captain Zero	
A presses + $0 + 0 = 0$	B presses − B says, "Instruction A" $4120000 - 0 = 4120000$	C presses × $0 \times 0 = 0$

A	B	C
		C is Captain Zero
A presses +	B presses ÷	C presses ÷
		C says, "Instruction C"
0 + 100 = 100	4120000 ÷ 100 = 41200	0 ÷ 100 = 0
A is Captain Zero		
A presses ×	B presses ÷	C presses ×
A says, "Instruction D"		
100 × 100 = 10000	41200 ÷ 41200 = 1	0 × 0 = 0
A wins.		

CHAPTER SIX:
Multiplying Is
Adding Faster

Multiplying one number by another number is a fast method of addition. For example: 6×3 means $6 + 6 + 6$, six added three times. Your calculator speeds up multiplication.

THE MULTIPLICATION TARGET

Begin in the middle of the target at "1" and work out. You must figure out what number multiplied by what other number results in the number in the ring. For example: for 1, only $1 \times 1 = 1$. That's the answer.

All the numbers you may multiply with are between 1 and 9. What times what equals 2? Some of the numbers can be arrived at by more than one possibility. For example: $4 \times 6 = 24$, and $8 \times 3 = 24$. Figure out all the possibilities. Check all your answers.

THE MULTIPLICATION TARGET

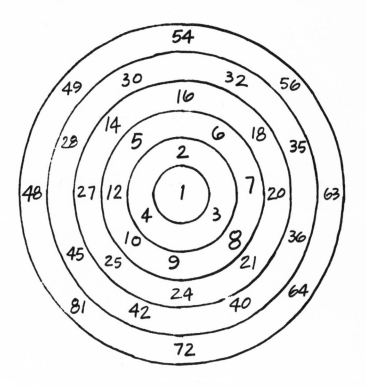

FIVE HIGH

2 Players
2 Calculators
Dice

OBJECT OF THE GAME

To have the highest number after each player has had ten turns to say an operation and a number.

THE PLAY

Each player rolls 1 die and enters that number in his/her calculator. Player A rolls die and says an operation ($+$, $-$, $\times$, $\div$). For example: A rolls 6 and says, "Add 6." Both players follow this instruction.

If the result is

1. evenly divisible by 2, multiply by 2.

2. a Prime Number, multiply by that number (a Prime Number is a number which is divisible only by itself; 17 is a Prime Number, for example. See Prime Chapter).

3. evenly divisible by 3, subtract 3.

4. evenly divisible by 5, add 5.

Player B says an operation and rolls both dice and says the number. The players follow the instructions and then consult the above list. If a number is divisible by 2, 3, or 5, the player has to decide what to do. Remember, the player with the highest score after each player has said an operation and a number ten times is the winner.

This game is a fast game. A good match would be the best two out of three games.

SAMPLE PLAY

A	B
Rolls 5	Rolls 6
A enters 5	B enters 6
A rolls dice, gets 4	
A says, "Add 4"	
$5 + 4 = 9$	$6 + 4 = 10$
9 is evenly divisible by 3	10 is evenly divisible by 2 and 5;
so $9 - 3 = 6$	B chooses $10 \times 2 = 20$
	B rolls dice, gets 9
	B says, "Multiply by 9"
$6 \times 9 = 54$	$20 \times 9 = 180$
54 is evenly divisible by 2 and 3	180 is evenly divisible by 2, 3, and 5
so chooses $54 \times 2 = 108$	so chooses $180 \times 2 = 360$

The play continues for eight more rounds.

1000000

3 or More Players
1 Calculator per Player
Dice

OBJECT OF THE GAME
To be the last player to go over 1000000.

THE PLAY
Each player enters a two-digit number, no digits the same. The players each roll the dice. High roll goes first, second highest second, etc.

Player A rolls the dice twice. Player A can either add the total to his/her number, *or* multiply by both numbers. For example: Player A enters 56 and then rolls 12 and 6. Player A can add 18 (56 + 18 = 74) or multiply by 12 and then 6 (56 × 12 = 672 × 6 = 4032). A player cannot add one number and multiply by the other number. The player must either add both or multiply by both. Players cannot *add* more than five turns in a row.

The second player follows the same procedure. The game continues until all but one player have gone over 1000000.

SAMPLE PLAY

A enters 45

rolls dice
gets 8
goes second

B enters 96

gets 11
goes first

rolls dice twice
gets 7 and 11

decides to multiply
by both numbers

$96 \times 7 = 672 \times 11 = 7392$

C enters 13

gets 6
goes third

rolls dice twice
gets 8 and 8

decides to multiply
by both numbers

$45 \times 8 = 360 \times 8 = 2880$

rolls dice twice
gets 5 and 8

decides to multiply
by both numbers

$13 \times 5 = 65 \times 8 = 520$

A rolls dice twice
gets 11 and 6

decides to multiply
by both numbers

$2880 \times 11 = 31680 \times 6 = 190080$

B rolls dice twice
gets 8 and 4

decides to multiply
by both numbers

$7392 \times 8 = 59136 \times 4 = 236544$

C rolls dice twice
gets 3 and 7

decides to multiply
by both numbers

$520 \times 3 = 1560 \times 7 = 10920$

B rolls dice twice
gets 4 and 5

decides to add
both numbers

$236544 + 4 + 5 = 236553$

A rolls dice twice
gets 2 and 6

decides to multiply
by both numbers

$190080 \times 2 = 380160 \times 6 = 2280960$

goes over 1000000

B rolls dice twice
gets 2 and 3

decides to multiply
by both numbers

$236553 \times 2 = 473106$
$473106 \times 3 = 1419318$

goes over 1000000

C rolls dice twice
gets 7 and 11

decides to multiply by
both numbers

$10920 \times 7 = 76440 \times 11 = 840840$

Player C wins since
is still under 1000000

CHAPTER SEVEN:
Hidden Multiplier

Pressing a number button on the calculator is really doing two operations. When you press 9 you are adding 9 to the calculator and multiplying by 1. When you press 9 again you are multiplying 9×10 and then adding it to 9. When you press the 9 again you are multiplying 9×100 and adding it to 99. The same would be true if you wrote 9 and then wrote 9 to the left of that and 9 to the left of that. This is simply a form of noting down numbers which makes it easier to use them. It would be very hard to note down numbers in the older, more primitive ways like:

$$\text{卅} \quad \text{卅} \quad \text{卅} \quad \text{卅} \quad = \quad 20$$

where the diagonal line groups the 4 lines into a group of 5. How would you multiply these? Or add them? You would have a hard time. The ABACUS is organized like the calculator and like our ARABIC number system (so named because it was invented by an Arabian mathematician more than 2,000 years ago). Our number system is very efficient, but the efficiency of it is sometimes hidden as in the hidden multiplication and addition that was described above. The following puzzle may make this "hidden multiplier" more obvious to you.

HIDDEN MULTIPLIER PUZZLE

You want the number on your calculator to be the largest possible after playing five turns. A turn can either be:

Method 1: Press a number button (although none of the numbers may be pressed more than once. You can't press all 9's), or

Method 2: Press a number button (not using a number more than once) AND press the multiplication button.

Once you decide to use Method 1 or Method 2 you *must continue to use only that method for five turns.*

Once you have done this with the Method you selected, try the other Method and compare the results. *You will always get a larger number using Method 1.* This is because you are multiplying AND adding and because you are multiplying by larger and larger numbers each time you press another button. For example: In pressing 98765 you are multiplying 1×5 and then adding it to the calculator, then 6×10 and adding it, then 7×100 and adding it, then 8×1000 and adding it and then 9×10000 and adding it. When you multiply with one-digit numbers you are only multiplying by them and are getting no "hidden multiplier."

HIDDEN MULTIPLIER GAME

2 Players
2 Calculators
Dice

OBJECT OF THE GAME
To have the largest number after ten rounds.

THE PLAY
Each player rolls the dice. The player with the largest number goes first. Player A (the first Player) rolls the dice and enters that number. Then Player B rolls the dice and enters that number. Now Player A rolls the dice again. If the number is EVEN (2,4,6,8,10, 12), Player A multiplies by that number. If it is ODD (3,5,7,9,11), then Player A enters that number. Then Player B goes and does the same. That is one round. The player with the largest number after ten rounds is the winner.

SAMPLE PLAY

Player A	Player B
Rolls 8	Rolls 6
Rolls 12 enters 12	Rolls 9 enters 9
Rolls 2 (even) 12 × 2 = 24	Rolls 7 (odd) enters 7 = 97
Rolls 3 (odd) enters 3 = 243	Rolls 6 (even) 97 × 6 = 582
Rolls 11 (odd) enters 11 = 24311	Rolls 10 (even) 582 × 10 = 5820

Play continues for six more rounds. The player with the largest number wins.

THE DICE GAME

3 or More Players
1 Calculator per Player
Dice

OBJECT OF THE GAME

To have the highest number after each player has rolled the dice ten times.

THE PLAY

Each player rolls one die only to see who goes first. High roll goes first, second highest second, etc.

Player A rolls the dice and enters the number that appears. Player B, Player C, etc., do the same in turn.

Player A now rolls the dice again and consults the chart as to what to do:

> Roll 2, then multiply by 2
> Roll 3, then add 3
> Roll 4, then press 4 (no operation)
> Roll 5, then multiply by 5
> Roll 6, then add 6
> Roll 7, then subtract 7
> Roll 8, then multiply by 8
> Roll 9, then add 9
> Roll 10, then press 10 (no operation)
> Roll 11, then divide by 11
> Roll 12, then multiply by 12

Each player takes a turn rolling the dice and doing what the chart instructs. The players continue until each player has rolled the dice ten times. The player with the highest score wins.

SAMPLE PLAY

A	B	C	D
rolls die	rolls die	rolls die	rolls die
gets 3	gets 6	gets 5	gets 2
enters 3	enters 6	enters 5	enters 2
A goes third	B goes first	C goes second	D goes fourth

B rolls dice
gets 7
must subtract 7
$6 - 7 = -1$

C rolls dice
gets 6
must add 6
$5 + 6 = 11$

A rolls dice
gets 10
must press 10
with no operation
entry reads 310

D rolls dice
gets 4
must press 4
with no operation
entry reads 24

The play continues until each player has rolled the dice ten times. The player with the highest score wins.

CHAPTER EIGHT:
Paradox Appears

A paradox is something that seems contrary to common sense and yet is true. Using numbers and calculators can result in paradoxes, but they usually can be understood if they are investigated. Let's investigate a paradox discovered by the philosopher Zeno 2,000 years ago.

PARADOX PUZZLE

In order to do this puzzle, you need a calculator and a tape measure.

Measure the room you are in very accurately, by measuring from the middle of one wall over to the middle of the opposite wall, and then measuring from the middle of the adjacent wall to the middle of the wall opposite.

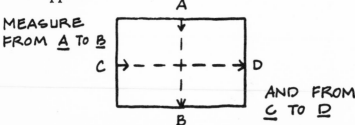

MEASURE
FROM A TO B

C $\rightarrow$ — — + — — $\rightarrow$ D

A

B

AND FROM
C TO D

Make sure that you get the smallest fraction of the distance, for instance, 20 feet, 5.6 inches. Now, convert the measurements to inches: $20 \times 12 = 240$ inches $+$ 5.6 inches $= 245.6$ inches. If the inches are in $\frac{1}{2}$ or $\frac{1}{4}$, you must change them to their decimal value: $\frac{1}{2}$ inch $= .5$; $\frac{1}{4}$ inch $= .25$; $\frac{1}{8}$ inch $= .125$; $\frac{1}{16}$ inch $= .0625$. If you have $\frac{3}{4}$ inch, multiply $.25 \times 3 = .75$.

Stand on one side of the room, with the measurements on a piece of paper. Divide the distance between you and the wall opposite you by 2 (this is like halving the distance), using your calculator. Now measure that distance away from the wall and move to that point. Subtract the distance you moved from the original measurements and from this new point, measure that distance, divide it in half again (divide by 2), and move to that point. Now subtract that amount from the total distance of the room and continue the process, until you get across the room. Stop reading now and try it.

You cannot get across the room completely because you will always be moving only HALF the distance to it! You will get very close, but not all the way.

What would happen if you divided by 3 or 4 each time instead of by 2? You would move one-third of the distance or one-quarter of the distance.

Since you measured the room in both directions, move across it in the other direction dividing the number by one-third this time.

TORTOISE AND HARE

2 Players
2 Calculators
Dice

OBJECT OF THE GAME
To get over 200 before the other player.

THE PLAY
Each player rolls the dice. The player with the highest number is the HARE, the other player is the TORTOISE. The Hare then rolls the dice and enters the number rolled; the Tortoise rolls the dice and enters the number rolled.

The Hare rolls again and multiplies by the number rolled. The Tortoise rolls the dice and adds twice the number rolled. Now the Hare goes again but this time the Hare multiplies by $\frac{1}{2}$ the number rolled (if the Hare rolls 6, multiplies by 3). The Tortoise rolls the dice and adds twice the number rolled to the total.

On each following round, the Hare multiplies by $\frac{1}{4}$, then $\frac{1}{8}$, then $\frac{1}{16}$, then $\frac{1}{32}$, then $\frac{1}{64}$, then $\frac{1}{128}$, then $\frac{1}{256}$, then $\frac{1}{512}$, and so on, of the number rolled. And the Tortoise adds twice the number rolled each time. The first player to get over 200 wins the game.

SAMPLE PLAY

Tortoise	Hare
Rolls 6 enters 6	Rolls 9 enters 9
Rolls 7, enters $6 + 14 = 20$	Rolls 4, $9 \times 4 = 36$
Rolls 4, enters $20 + 8 = 28$	Rolls 4 ($\frac{1}{2}$ 4 = 2) $36 \times 2 = 72$
Rolls 12, enters $28 + 24 = 52$	Rolls 8 ($\frac{1}{4}$ 8 = 2) $72 \times 2 = 144$

and so on until one player gets over 200.

TWO MUCH

3 or More Players
1 Calculator per Player
Pencil and Paper

OBJECT OF THE GAME

To predict accurately how many times a number can be divided by 2 with the result being between 1 and 0, and have the lowest result.

THE PLAY

Each player enters a six-digit number in his/her calculator, no digits the same. They do not show this number to each other. Now each player guesses how many times that number can be divided by 2 so that the result will be less than 1 and greater than 0. For example, a result of .5 would be good. Each player writes his/her guess on a piece of paper which is placed so that everyone can see it.

Now each player divides by 2 the number of times they guessed. For example: If Player A says he/she will divide by 2 twelve times, then Player A divides by 2 twelve times and stops. If the result is between 1 and 0, A gets one point. Once all the players have divided, they compare results. The player with the lowest result between 1 and 0 *gets an additional point.* For example, if Player A has .8 as the result, and Player B has .005, then Player B gets an additional point. If none of the players has a result between 1 and 0, then nobody gets a point.

Each player makes up a new six-digit number for each round and makes a new prediction. Play continues for seven rounds. The player with the most points wins.

SAMPLE PLAY
Player A enters 453861
Guesses that it can be divided by 2, 20 times

Player B enters 123456
Guesses that it can be divided by 2, 12 times

Player C enters 756940
Guesses that it can be divided by 2, 40 times

Player A calculates
453861 divided by 2, 20 times
The result is .4328355
A's result is between 1 and 0. Gets 1 point.

Player B calculates
123456 divided by 2, 12 times
The result is 30.140625
B's answer is not between 1 and 0
B gets no points.

Player C calculates
756940 divided by 2, 40 times
The result is .0000006
C's result is between 1 and 0. Gets 1 point.
C's result is the lowest and gets 1 more point.

The play continues with each player entering a new six-digit number and making a prediction of how many times it can be divided by 2.

CHAPTER NINE:
Being Above Average

If there are two kids in a room and they want to know what their average age is, they add their ages together and divide by two. For example: If one kid is 9 and the other is 11, then $9 + 11 = 20 \div 2 = 10$, so 10 is their average age.

An average is the number which is halfway between two numbers or equidistant from three numbers. For example: The average of the numbers 5, 8, and 80 is $5 + 8 + 80 = 93 \div 3 = 31$. An average can be a whole number or a number that has a decimal part. For example: The average of 7 and 8 is 7.5 ($7 + 8 = 15 \div 2 = 7.5$).

AVERAGE PUZZLE

Your number is 1. You want to get halfway between 1 and 2 (1.5) without using addition. You have at most three turns in which to do it. A turn consists of pressing a number key and an operation ($+$, $-$, $\times$, $\div$). There are at least four ways to do it in two turns.

—OR—

Your number is 2. You want to get halfway between 2 and 1 (1.5) without using subtraction. You have at most three turns to do it. If you do it in two turns, you're a champ. There are at least four ways to do it in three turns.

HALF-TIME

2 Players
2 Calculators
Dice

OBJECT OF THE GAME

To get exactly halfway between the two chosen numbers in the fewest turns.

THE PLAY

Each player rolls the dice and enters the number in his/her calculator. The players add the two numbers together and divide the result by 2. This is the *Average Number*. If the Average Number is a decimal number (for example: $6 + 5 = 11 \div 2 = 5.5$), then the players cannot use a decimal number when they add or subtract. If the Average Number is a whole number ($6 + 8 = 14 \div 2 = 7$), then the players may not use whole numbers when they add or subtract during the game. *The player who rolls the larger number cannot use subtraction during the round, and the player with the lower number cannot use addition.*

Once the Average Number is determined, then Player A goes. Player A says a number and an operation trying to get to the Average Number. Player A uses this operation and number with the original number that Player A rolled. For example: If Player A rolled 9 and then said, "Multiply by 7," then Player A would multiply by 7 ($7 \times 9 = 63$). Then Player B goes. Player B says an operation and a number and uses it with Player B's original number. Player A goes again and so on until one of the players reaches the Average Number exactly.

REMEMBER, if the Average Number is a decimal, then neither player may use decimal numbers in addition or subtraction trying to get the Average Number. And if the Average Number is a whole number, players may not use whole numbers in addition or subtraction, trying to get to the Average Number.

The player who gets the Average Number first, gets one point. If a player uses neither addition nor subtraction to get the Average Number and wins, that player gets two points. The first player to get ten points is the Average Champ.

SAMPLE PLAY

A	B
enters 3	enters 8
$3 + 8 = 11 \div 2 = 5.5$	$8 + 3 = 11 \div 2 = 5.5$

5.5 is the Average Number

Neither player can use a decimal number in addition or subtraction since the Average Number is a decimal number.

A cannot use addition during round because he/she entered the lower number	B cannot use subtraction during round because he/she entered the higher number
A starts to calculate	
$3 \times 4 = 12$	
	B calculates
	$8 \div 2 = 4$
A calculates	
$12 - 1 = 11$	
	B calculates
	$4 \times 5 = 20$
A calculates	
$11 \div 2 = 5.5$	
	B calculates
	$20 + 2 = 22$
	$22 \div 4 = 5.5$
A used 3 turns	B used 4 turns

A wins the round
gets 1 point

The game continues with the players selecting new numbers for the next round. The player who gets ten points total wins the game.

THE GUESSING GAME

3 or More Players
1 Calculator per Player
Pencil and Paper

OBJECT OF THE GAME
To have the fewest points after ten rounds.

THE PLAY
Each player enters a two-digit number in the calculator, no digit the same, presses the multiplication key, and enters another two-digit number, no digits the same. For example: 78 × 34 = 2652. The result (2652) is the Player's Averaging Number (AN).

Each player now says his/her AN out loud. The other players write these AN numbers down and WITHOUT USING THEIR CALCULATORS, and within 20 seconds, make a guess as to the Average Number of all the AN's. Each player writes down his/her Guess Number.

Each player now adds all the AN's together on his/her calculator and divides the total by the number of players to find out what the Average Number of the AN's actually is. Each player then finds out the difference between his/her Guess Number and the actual Average Number. This is the player's score for that round.

Each player now enters another two-digit number, no digits the same, presses the multiplication key and enters another two-digit number, no digits the same. The game continues for ten rounds. The player with the LOWEST total score after ten rounds wins.

SAMPLE PLAY

A enters
21 × 15 = 315
315 is A's AN

B enters
79 × 34 = 2686
2686 is B's AN

C enters
10 × 82 = 820
820 is C's AN

Now each player says out loud his or her AN

Player A says
315

Player B says
2686

Player C says
820

Player A now
writes Guess Number:

Player B now
writes Guess Number:

Player C now
writes Guess Number:

1800

1300

1100

Now each of the players writes down all the AN's and then they calculate what the real Average Number is:

315 + 2686 + 820 = 3821

3821 ÷ 3 = 1273.66 The Average Number

Now each player calculates the difference between his/her Guess Number and the Average Number.

Player A's Guess Number was
1800 — 1273.66 = 526.34
A's score for this round.

Player B's Guess Number was
1300 — 1273.66 = 26.34
B's score for this round.

Player C's Guess Number was
1100 — 1273.66 = 173.66
C's score for this round.

The game continues in this manner with each player finding a new Averaging Number (AN) and so on. The player with the lowest total score after 10 rounds wins the game.

CHAPTER TEN:
Subtracting Without Losing

To reduce a number to a lower number, you subtract from it. Often, it is easy to estimate what to subtract from a number to get the desired result. For example: You want 10 and have 20. You can easily guess to subtract 10. But, if you have a six-digit number like 654321 and want to reduce it to 15, and can subtract only three-digit numbers at a time, it is not so easy to know what to do.

THE SUBTRACTING PUZZLE

The object of the Subtracting Puzzle is to reduce a six-digit number to exactly zero.

Enter a six-digit number in the calculator, no digits the same, and with numbers in descending order from left to right. For example: 654321, or 987632, or 875430. Now, by subtracting only five-digit numbers, reduce the number to exactly zero. You will run into trouble if you wind up with a four-digit number after any of your calculations. This means that your next subtraction will result in a number below zero.

THE NOTHING GAME

2 Players
2 Calculators

OBJECT OF THE GAME

To reduce your number to zero in the fewest number of subtractions.

THE PLAY

Both players enter the same six-digit number in their calculators, no digits the same, and the digits in descending order from left to right. Each player proceeds from this number, trying to get exactly zero.

The players must subtract five-digit numbers before subtracting four-digit numbers before subtracting three-digit numbers before subtracting two-digit numbers. For example: If a player subtracts five-digit numbers, the player must then subtract four-digit numbers, then three-digit numbers, and so on. A player may not subtract a five-digit number again, once the player has subtracted a four-digit number. A player may not subtract a five-digit number and then a three-digit number, or two-digit number, but must subtract four-digit numbers, then three-digit, etc. For example: If a player subtracted five-digit numbers so that all that remained was 23, the player loses since the player can't subtract a four-digit number from 23 without going below zero.

The player who subtracts and gets the lowest number in the fewest turns and does not go below zero is the winner. The player who wins three out of five rounds wins the game.

SAMPLE PLAY

Players decide together on 753210

	753210			753210
Player A subtracts	53210		Player B subtracts	99999
	= 700000			= 653211
then subtracts	99990		then subtracts	99999
	= 600010			= 553212
then subtracts	99910		then subtracts	90000
	= 500100			= 463212
then subtracts	99100		then subtracts	63000
	= 401000			= 400212
then subtracts	91999		then subtracts	90000
	= 309001			= 310212
then subtracts	99001		then subtracts	80000
	= 210000			= 230212
then subtracts	90000		then subtracts	90000
	= 120000			= 140212
then subtracts	90000		then subtracts	90000
	= 30000			= 50212
then subtracts	30000		then subtracts	50000
	= 0			= 212

Player B now must subtract a four-digit number before he can subtract a three-digit number, so he automatically loses.

Player A finishes in nine turns.

Player A wins this round and the players select a new number and continue.

TAKE AWAY

4 or More Players
1 Calculator per Player

OBJECT OF THE GAME
To win the game by winning five rounds with the highest number.

THE PLAY
Each player enters a six-digit number in his/her calculator, no digits the same, and the numbers in descending order from left to right (i.e., 654321). The players take turns being the Subtractor. The Subtractor says, "Take away your 5's" (or any other number chosen). Each player must subtract the VALUE of the number that the Subtractor states from their number. For example: If Player A had 654321, and the Subtractor says, "Take away your 2's," then Player A would subtract 20 from 654321: $654321 - 20 = 654301$. If the number called does not appear in a player's number, the player does not subtract and the number remains unchanged.

After a player says a number as the Subtractor, another player becomes the Subtractor. Remember, the Subtractor must also subtract the number that he or she calls from his or her own number. Therefore, a smart Subtractor will not call a number he has. The Subtractor may say any number between 1 and 9 even if it has already been said.

After each player has been the Subtractor once, the player with the highest score wins the round. The players now enter a new six-digit number, no digits the same and in descending order, but *with a different Lead Digit*. The first player to win five rounds wins the game.

SAMPLE PLAY

A	B	C	D
enters 985432	enters 754310	enters 543210	enters 863210

A is Subtractor says, "Take away your 6's"

A	B	C	D
985432 stays the same	754310 stays the same	543210 stays the same	863210 − 60000 = 803210

B is Subtractor says, "Take away your 2's"

A	B	C	D
985432 − 2 = 985430	754310 stays the same	543210 − 200 = 543010	803210 − 200 = 803010

C is Subtractor
says,
"Take away your 8's"

803010
—800000
3010

D is Subtractor
says,
"Take away your 7's"

543010
stays the same

3010
stays the same

754310
stays the same

543010
stays the same

754310
—700000
54310

985430
— 80000
905430

905430
stays the same

Player A wins the round.

The game continues with all players entering new six-digit numbers. The first player to win five rounds wins the game.

CHAPTER ELEVEN:
Conquering and Dividing

When you divide one number by another number, you discover how many times a number is included in another number. For example: If you multiply 2 × 4 you get 8; if you divide 8 by 4 you get 2, which means that 2 is included 4 times in 8. Sometimes a number divided into another number is not included a whole number of times. For example: If you multiply 6 × 1.5 you get 9; if you divide 9 by 6 you get 1.5, which means that 6 is included 1.5 times in 9. The 1.5 is called a decimal result. Sometimes it is easy to tell if a number can be evenly divided by another number with no decimal result; other times, it is not so easy.

To divide, do the following: You want to divide 648 by 8. First look to see if 8 is included in the Lead Digit, 6. It is not. Now try the first two digits, 64: 8 is included in 64, 8 times. Next, look at the next digit, 8: 8 is included in 8, once. The answer to how many times 8 is included in 648 is 81 (648 ÷ 8 = 81).

THE DIVIDING BOX

If you divide a number in the left column by one of the numbers in the right column of the Dividing Box, you will get another number in the left column as a result. Begin with 362880 and keep dividing until the readout on the calculator is 1.

DIVIDING BOX

1 (FINISH)	9
432	2
60480	3
362880 (START)	5
181440	8
12096	4
3024	7
72	6
9	

SECRET NUMBER

2 Players
2 Calculators

OBJECT OF THE GAME

To have the largest number not exceeding 9999 after five rounds.

THE PLAY

Players have calculators concealed. Each player enters a two-digit number, no digits the same, and presses the divide key. Player A says a number between

1 and 9, and both players enter it and press the equal key. Now both players press the multiplication key, and Player B says a number between 1 and 9. Both players enter it and press the equal key.

Next, both players press the divide key, and Player A says another number between 1 and 9, and the game continues until both players have said five numbers. The players may say any number between 1 and 9 any number of times. The players must alternate between division and multiplication each round.

HOWEVER: After the players have each said two numbers, for the next three rounds they may ADD A SECRET NUMBER TO THEIR TOTAL. This Secret Number is determined by reversing the first two digits of the number on the player's own calculator. For example: Player A has *236* so A may add 32. This addition can be done twice during the next three rounds. The players must remember that THEIR TOTAL MAY NOT EXCEED 9999 after five rounds. If a player goes over 9999, the player automatically loses. The player with the largest number after five rounds wins the game.

SAMPLE PLAY

A enters 34 ÷	B enters 19 ÷
A says, "2"	
34 ÷ 2 = 17	19 ÷ 2 = 9.5
press ×	press ×
	says, "8"
17 × 8 = 136	9.5 × 8 = 76

press ÷	press ÷
says, "2"	
136 ÷ 2 = 68	76 ÷ 2 = 38
press ×	press ×
	says, "9"
68 × 9 = 612	38 × 9 = 342

press ÷	press ÷
says, "1"	
612 ÷ 1 = 612	342 ÷ 1 = 342
press ×	press ×
	says, "3"
612 × 3 = 1836	342 × 3 = 1026
A adds Secret Number	
1836 + 81 = 1917	

press ÷	press ÷
says, "1"	
1917 ÷ 1 = 1917	1026 ÷ 1 = 1026
press ×	press ×
	says, "9"
1917 × 9 = 17253	1026 × 9 = 9234
	B adds Secret Number
A has gone over 9999	9234 + 29 = 9263

B wins game.

THE TENTH DIVISION

3 or More Players
1 Calculator per Player
Pencil and Paper
Dice

OBJECT OF THE GAME
For all players to have the same number in their calculators after ten rounds of divisions.

THE PLAY
Each player enters a six-digit number, no digits the same. The players roll the dice to see who goes first.

Highest roll goes first, second highest second, etc. Player A then rolls the dice and divides his/her number by the numbers on the dice and gives the result to Player B, who writes it down. Player A subtracts this division from his/her original number. Player A rolls the dice again and does the same thing with Player C, and so on until Player A has given a number to each of the players. For example: Player A enters 654320 and rolls 5. $654320 \div 5 = 130864$. Player A subtracts this from his number and gives 130864 to Player B. Player A now has $654320 - 130864 = 523456$. Player A rolls the dice and gets 2; $523456 \div 2 = 261728$. Player A gives 261728 to Player C and subtracts it: $523456 - 261728 = 261728$.

Player A thus gives one number to all players, saying the number out loud, and each player writes down the number given to him/her.

Player B does the same, and so on, until all the players have rolled the dice and distributed the results to the other players.

The players then add the totals of the numbers given to them, plus what remains on their calculator. The players compare results. If the totals are exactly the same, they have succeeded. If their numbers are within 100 of each other, they have done well. More than 100 apart, play again.

SAMPLE PLAY

A enters 123456

A goes first

rolls dice
gets 5

$123456 \div 5 = 24691.2$
gives it to C

C enters 246801

C goes second

C writes 24691.2

B enters 579642

B goes third

$123456 — 24691.2 = 98764.8$

Rolls dice
gets 9

$98764.8 \div 9 = 10973.866$
gives it to B

B writes 10973.866

$98764.8 — 10973.866 = 87790.934$
(keeps this)

C rolls dice
gets 11

$246801 \div 11 = 22436.454$
gives it to B

B writes 22436.454

$246801 — 22436.454 = 224364.55$

rolls dice
gets 7

$224364.55 \div 7 = 32052.078$
gives it to A

101

A writes 32052.078

$224364.55 - 32052.078 = 192312.48$

B rolls dice
gets 6

$579642 \div 6 = 96607$
gives it to A

A writes 96607

$579642 - 96607 = 483035$

rolls dice
gets 4

$483035 \div 4 = 120758.75$
gives it to C

C writes 120758.75

$483035 - 120758.75 = 362276.25$

The play continues with A rolling the dice to start round two.

CHAPTER TWELVE:
Parts of Wholes:
Fractions and Decimals

The number 4 can be expressed or written as fractions, $\frac{8}{2}$ or $\frac{16}{4}$, which means that the top number divided by the bottom number equals 4: $8 \div 2 = 4$ and $16 \div 4 = 4$. Your pocket calculator cannot show fractions, but it can show the equivalent to a fraction, i.e., 4, the result of a fraction.

A number that is less than 1 and greater than 0 can be written as a fraction, for example, $\frac{1}{2}$. To enter this in your calculator, divide the top number by the bottom number, $1 \div 2 = .5$. Instead of entering $\frac{1}{2}$ in your calculator which you cannot do, you can enter the equivalent, .5. Decimal numbers are the result of the division of fractions.

FRACTIONS-TO-DECIMALS PUZZLE

In this puzzle, figure out which fraction results in the decimal numbers in the boxes by dividing the top number by the bottom number. The decimal numbers in the boxes correspond to a fraction in the list below. You must associate one fraction with one decimal number doing the puzzle from start to finish. Notice that some of the fractions are followed by several fractions in parentheses, i.e., ½ (²/₄) (⅘). The fractions in the parentheses are equivalent to the fraction preceding them: ½ = ²/₄ = ⅘; therefore you must find the decimal number which corresponds to ½, since it will be the same one for ²/₄ and ⅘.

Decimal numbers are rounded off, which means reduced to fewer places than they would actually have, in two ways: they are rounded off to the higher number if the last digit is 5 or more, and to the lower number if the last digit is 4 or less. For example, .11116 is rounded off to .1112, and .11114 is rounded off to .1111. In this chart .11111111 is rounded off to .111111 because most calculators only have 6 places; and .77777777 is rounded off to .777778.

FRACTIONS-TO-DECIMALS PUZZLE

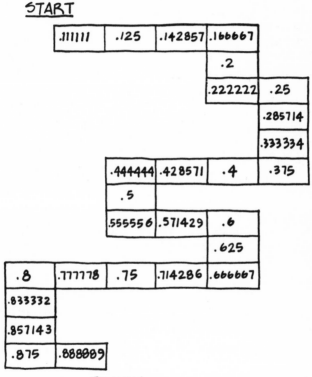

START

FINISH

Fractions List:

These are the fractions to use to get the above numbers: ½ (²⁄₄) (⁴⁄₈), ⅓ (²⁄₆) (³⁄₉), ¼ (²⁄₈), ⅕, ⅙, ⅐, ⅛, ⅑, ⅔ (⁴⁄₆) (⁶⁄₉), ⅖, ²⁄₇, ²⁄₉, ¾ (⁶⁄₈), ⅗, ³⁄₇, ⅜, ⅘, ⁴⁄₇, ⁴⁄₉, ⅚, ⁵⁄₇, ⅝, ⁵⁄₉, ⁶⁄₇, ⅞, ⁷⁄₉, ⁸⁄₉

TRANSFORMATION

2 Players
1 Calculator per Player
Pencil and Paper
Watch

OBJECT OF THE GAME

To get more than 8.75 by adding up fractions converted into decimals.

THE PLAY

Each player looks at the Fractions-to-Decimals Puzzle on page 105. Player A says one of the fractions, such as ⅔. Player B must then transform this into the decimal number to which it is equivalent. Player B has 10 seconds to do this. If B does not complete it, then B can't write it down. If Player B does complete it, then Player B writes down the fraction and the decimal value.

Player B says a fraction, of which Player A must find the decimal equivalent in less than 10 seconds. NO FRACTION CAN BE SAID MORE THAN ONCE.

The game continues until all 35 fractions have been used. The players then add together the decimal equivalents they have written down. The player who reaches 8.75 or more is the winner. If both players have more than 8.75, someone has made a mistake. Double-check the fraction-to-decimal equivalents.

SAMPLE PLAY

Player A says, "⅖"

Player B calculates
2 ÷ 5 = .4
within 10-second limit
writes .4

B says, "¾"

A calculates
3 ÷ 4 = .75
within 10-second limit
writes .75

A says, "⅓"

B calculates
1 ÷ 3 = .333333
within 10-second limit
writes .333333

B says, "⅑"

A calculates
1 ÷ 9 = .111111
within 10-second limit
writes .111111

A says, "⅕"

B calculates
1 ÷ 5 = .2
within 10-second limit
writes .2

B says, "2/7"

A calculates
2 ÷ 7 = .285714
within 10-second limit
writes .285714

A says ,"⅐"

B mistakenly calculates
7 ÷ 1 and has to clear and
reenter 1 ÷ 7; goes over
10-second limit and cannot
write decimal down to
add to score

B says, "2/9"

A calculates
2 ÷ 9 = .222222
within 10-second limit
writes .222222

Score after 4 rounds
A has 1.369047   B has .933333

The game continues until one of the players reaches 8.75 or more.

"I GOT IT!"

3 or More Players
1 Calculator per Player
Pencil and Paper
Watch

OBJECT OF THE GAME

To calculate the correct decimal equivalents to fractions in the fastest time.

THE PLAY

This is a game of speed and accuracy.

Each player takes a turn being the Converter. The Converter makes up a series of three complex fractions (a complex fraction is made up of a whole number *and* a fraction, for example: $3\frac{1}{2}$ or $4\frac{1}{4}$) and two operations, writes them down, and shows them to the other players. Each player (including the Converter) tries to transform the fractions into decimals and then do the operations. For example: the Converter writes $3\frac{1}{2} \times 9\frac{1}{4} + 6\frac{7}{8}$.

The first player to complete the operations says, "I got it!" The other players stop what they are doing, and the first player tells the answer. The others check this answer. If it is correct, the player who "got it" gets one point. If it is incorrect, the player gets minus one point. Another player then becomes the Converter. The first player to get ten points wins the game.

SAMPLE PLAY

A is the Converter

makes up $81/2 + 33/4 \times 42/7$

and shows to other players

A calculates

$1/2 = 1 \div 2 = .5$

so $81/2 = 8.5$

$3/4 = 3 \div 4 = .75$

so $33/4 = 3.75$

$2/7 = 2 \div 7 = .28571$

so $42/7 = 4.28571$

$8.5 + 3.75 \times 4.28571$

B calculates

$1/2 = 1 \div 2 = .5$

so $81/2 = 8.5$

$3/4 = 4 \div 3 = 1.33332$

so $33/4 = 4.33332$

$2/7 = 2 \div 7 = .28571$

so $42/7 = 4.28571$

$8.5 + 4.33332 \times 4.28571$

$= 54.9999$. Player B

says "I GOT IT"

C calculates

$1/2 = 1 \div 2 = .5$

$81/2 = 8.5$

$3/4 = 3 \div 4 = .75$

so $33/4 = 3.75$

$2/7 = 2 \div 7 = .28571$

so $42/7 = 4.28571$

$8.5 + 3.75 \ldots$

PLAY STOPS SINCE PLAYER B HAS SAID "I GOT IT"

A checks B

$8.5 + 3.75 \times 4.28571$
$= 52.4999$

C checks B

$8.5 + 3.75 \times 4.28571$
$= 52.4999$

A and C compare answers with B's answer.

B is WRONG (divided 4 by 3 rather than 3 by 4.) Player B gets −1 point.

Player A has 0   Player B has −1   Player C has 0

Game continues to next round with B as the Converter. Play continues until one player gets ten points and wins.

CHAPTER THIRTEEN:
Meaning of Mean

A Mean Number is a number that is between two numbers and is gotten by adding one number to the smaller of the two, then adding it again. For example: The Mean Number between 10 and 20 is 15. If we add 5 to 10 we get 15 and if we add 5 to 15 we get 20. The Mean Number is the intermediate number quantity between two numbers. There can also be more than one Mean Number between two numbers.

Between the numbers 10 and 25, there are two numbers that can be arrived at by adding a certain number to 10, then adding that number again to the result, and then adding it again to get 25. Can you figure out what this number is? You know that $25 - 10 = 15$, and that you must divide 15 into three parts since there is one number between 10 and the first number and one number between the first number and the second number, and one number between the second number and 25. If you divide 15 by $3 = 5$. So, $10 + 5 = 15 + 5 = 20 + 5 = 25$. The two numbers between 10 and 25 are 15 and 20.

These are the Mean Numbers. To get the Mean Numbers between two numbers, subtract the smaller number from the larger number. Then divide by ONE MORE THAN the number of Mean Numbers asked for. The result is the number you add to the smaller of the two numbers, and then add to the result of that to get the next Mean Number and so on, until you reach the larger of the two numbers.

THE MEAN PUZZLE BOX

The Mean Box is arranged so that the numbers which are the Mean Numbers in the following series are placed in rows or columns or on diagonals. Find the mean numbers of the following series, and then check the answer by finding that series in the Mean Box.

1. The 7 mean numbers between 10 and 50
2. The 9 mean numbers between 5 and 75
3. The 11 mean numbers between 3 and 99
4. The 6 mean numbers between 10 and 52
5. The 11 mean numbers between 5 and 11 (this one is a little harder since the mean numbers are decimals)

MEAN BOX

The Mean Numbers that you have been working with are called Arithmetic Mean Numbers. If you want to find a series that has numbers within that are arrived at by multiplying, these numbers are called Geometric Mean Numbers.

For example: There are five Geometric Mean Numbers between 7 and 448. To find out what they are, divide 448 by 7 = 64. Then you must find out what number, multiplied by itself 6 times, equals 64. (Notice that you still add 1 to the number of mean numbers as you did for Arithmetic Mean Numbers.) If you multiply 2 times itself 6 times, you get 64. $2 \times 2 \times 2 \times 2 \times 2 \times 2 = 64$. Then, you start with 7 and multiply it by 2, $7 \times 2 = 14$, and multiply that by 2, $14 \times 2 = 28$, and that by 2, $28 \times 2 = 56$, and that by 2, $56 \times 2 = 112$, and that by 2, $112 \times 2 = 224$, and that by 2, $224 \times 2 = 448$. So, 14, 28, 56, 112, and 224 are Geometric Mean Numbers.

Geometric Mean Numbers will be used in the game "Fast and Mean" at the end of this chapter.

8	3	7	4	11	86	52	21	32	69	46	102	114	11	25
2	4	8	17	9	11	46	22	86	40	60	23	69	71	80
1.5	5	12	19	26	33	40	47	54	61	68	75	6.2	7.3	8.4
9	5.5	7	6	5	4	34	3	2	1	13	14	15	16	7
8	6	1.1	1.3	1.5	2	28	7	91	19	18	22	11	4	99
8	6.5	7	2	111	43	22	8	9	11	16	22	31	91	4
9	7	3	0	1	99	16	4	45	1	10	9	83	8	97
9	7.5	7	0	9	3	10	4	19	6	6	75	73	7	94
8	8	1	9	10	12	13	11	17	15	67	99	5.6	6	92
7	8.5	5	2	8	5	14	14	16	59	42	5.5	4	5	91
33	9	6	7	6	16	42	43	51	77	82	4.1	2	3	87
2	9.5	11	50	66	48	41	43	68	79	23	61	18	11	42
5	10	15	20	25	30	35	40	45	50	1	2	3	4	63
14	10.5	9	6	3	27	1	2	1.6	1.8	1.9	2.1	2.7	6	11
9	11	14	17	19	82	63	62	61	60	59	58	1	2	22
1	1.2	16	11	5	15	18	19	20	22	24	26	28	30	18
6	12	3	18	21	27	29	37	86	85	84	83	82	81	21
3	6	9	12	15	18	21	24	27	29	31	32	33	34	9

MEAN BOX

MEAN NUMBER

2 Players
2 Calculators
Pencil and Paper
Watch

OBJECT OF THE GAME
To figure out the correct Mean Numbers.

THE PLAY
Each player calculates a number sequence between two numbers, writes the first and last numbers of the sequence and how many Mean Numbers there are between them. For example: A player calculates 2, 4, 6, 8, 10, 12, 14, 16, 18, 20, writes down 2 and 20, and that there are 8 Mean Numbers.

The players trade papers, and each player has three minutes to figure out the Mean Numbers. If the player gets it right, the player gets one point. If the player does not get it right, the player who wrote the sequence gets one point.

Play continues for ten rounds, and the player with the highest score wins.

SAMPLE PLAY

Player A uses the number sequence 1 4 7 10 13 16 19 22 25 28 31
to find that there are 9 mean numbers between 1 and 31.
A writes: 1 and 31 with 9 mean numbers
        and passes to B

Player B uses the number sequence 4 8 12 16 20 24
to find that there are 4 mean numbers between 4 and 24.
B writes: 4 and 24 with 4 mean numbers
        and passes to A

A calculates:
$24 - 4 = 20 \div 5 = 4$
$4 + 4 = 8 + 4 = 12 + 4 = 16 + 4 = 20 + 4 = 24$
8, 12, 16, 20 are the 4 mean numbers between 4 and 24.
A gets 1 point.

B calculates:
$31 - 1 = 30 \div 10 = 3$
$1 + 3 = 4 + 3 = 7 + 3 = 10 + 3 = 13 + 3 = 16 + 3 = 19 + 3 = 22 + 3 = 25 + 3 = 28 + 3 = 31$
4, 7, 10, 13, 16, 19, 22, 25, 28 are the 9 mean numbers between 1 and 31.
B gets 1 point.

The game continues in this manner until the player with the highest score after ten rounds wins.

FAST AND MEAN

3 or More Players
1 Calculator per Player
Pencil and Paper
Watch

OBJECT OF THE GAME

To figure out the Geometric Mean Numbers given to you.

THE PLAY

Each player invents a sequence of numbers between two numbers that are Geometric Means. Each player writes the first and last number, and the number of Geometric Mean Numbers on a piece of paper. Now, each player passes the paper to the player on the right. The players have three minutes to calculate the Geometric Mean Numbers. After three minutes are up, each player writes down his/her answer and passes the piece of paper back to the owner. If the answer is correct, the player gets one point. If the answer is wrong, the player who wrote the series gets one point.

Play continues for ten rounds. The player with the most points after ten rounds wins.

SAMPLE PLAY

A uses the sequence of numbers 6 18 54 162 486 1458
to find that there are 4 geometric means between 6 and 1458
A writes 6 and 1458
  4 geometric means and passes to B

B uses the sequence of numbers 1 2 4 8 16 32 64 128
to find that there are 6 geometric means between 1 and 128
B writes 1 and 128
  6 geometric means and passes to C

C uses the sequence of numbers 14 42 126 378
to find that there are 2 geometric means between 14 and 378
C writes 14 and 378
            2 geometric means and passes to A

A calculates
$378 \div 14 = 27$
figures what number times itself 3 times $= 27$
$3 \times 3 \times 3 = 27$
$14 \times 3 = 42 \times 3 = 126 \times 3 = 378$
42, 126 are the 2 geometric means between 14 and 378
A gets 1 point.

B calculates
$1458 \div 6 = 243$
figures what number times itself 5 times $= 243$
$3 \times 3 \times 3 \times 3 \times 3 = 243$
$6 \times 3 = 18 \times 3 = 54 \times 3 = 162 \times 3 = 486 \times 3 = 1458$
18, 54, 162, 486 are the 4 geometric means between 6 and 1458
but B goes over the three-minute time limit so
B gets no points.

C calculates
$128 \div 1 = 128$
figures what number times itself 7 times $= 128$
$2 \times 2 \times 2 \times 2 \times 2 \times 2 \times 2 = 128$
$1 \times 2 = 2 \times 2 = 4 \times 2 = 8 \times 2 = 16 \times 2 = 32 \times 2 = 64 \times 2 = 128$
2, 4, 8, 16, 32, 64 are the 6 geometric means between 1 and 128
C gets 1 point.

The game continues in this manner until ten rounds have been played, and the player with the highest number of points wins the game.

CHAPTER FOURTEEN:
Rational Ratios

A ratio is an expression of the relationship between two numbers. For example: You are climbing a hill on a road. Every 8 feet you walk along the road, the hill goes up 4 feet. The ratio would be 4 to 8, or ⅘, or 4 ÷ 8. How would you find out how far up the hill went if you walked 1 foot? Divide 4 by 8 = .5. The hill goes up .5 feet in 1 foot traveled on the road. The relationship gives you a way to understand the two numbers, 4 and 8, and therefore is called a ratio.

To make the ratio simpler, sometimes the numbers are divided by the same number, if possible to do it evenly, and the ratio is reduced, i.e., ⅘ is reduced to ½ by dividing both top and bottom numbers by 4.

When two numbers cannot be reduced evenly, this is an Irrational Number since we can't get it into a ratio that is reducible. For example, when you divide 100 by 3, you get 33.33333333333333333 . . . never ending. This is an irrational number. The ratio between the numbers is not whole (like 3, 5, 20, etc.).

RATIONAL MAZE PUZZLE

The Rational Maze is a puzzle that reveals the unexpected ratios between large numbers that can be gotten by dividing both top and bottom of the upper numbers in the boxes by the same number and reducing them to a number that can be found in one of the other boxes in the lower section. For example: If you divide $^{36}\!/_{72}$ by 2, you will get $^{18}\!/_{36}$, and if you divide that by 6, you will get $^3\!/_6$, and if you divide it again, you will get a ratio that exists as the lower ratio in one of the boxes. Once you get this, then calculate the upper ratio and proceed around the boxes until you get to $^1\!/_6$, the finish.

RATIONAL MAZE

START

$$\frac{36}{72}$$

$$\frac{1}{6}$$

FINISH

$$\frac{121}{1331}$$

$$\frac{1}{4}$$

$$\frac{512}{4096}$$

$$\frac{1}{5}$$

$$\frac{343}{2401}$$

$$\frac{1}{8}$$

$$\frac{125}{625}$$

$$\frac{1}{2}$$

$$\frac{729}{6561}$$

$$\frac{1}{11}$$

$$\frac{1728}{20736}$$

$$\frac{1}{9}$$

$$\frac{7776}{46656}$$

$$\frac{1}{12}$$

$$\frac{256}{1024}$$

$$\frac{1}{7}$$

123

TOP 20

2 Players
2 Calculators
Pencil and Paper

OBJECT OF THE GAME
To have the most points after ten rounds of play.

THE PLAY
Each player writes a line of twenty numbers of one or two digits across the top of a piece of paper, draws a line underneath them, and passes the paper to the other player. The other player writes a one- or two-digit number beneath the line under each of the numbers and passes it back to the original player.

Now the players divide the top numbers by the bottom numbers. If the result is a whole number, they get that number of points. For example: $6 \div 2 = 3 = 3$ points. If the result has a decimal value or is irrational (goes on forever like .3333333), then the player who wrote the bottom number loses ten points (-10 points). The players add their scores together for that round and then write a new line of twenty numbers, this time two- and three-digit numbers. The number of digits is increased each round until after the fifth round. So, in the first round, one- and two-digit numbers are used; in the second round, two- and three-digit numbers; in the third round, three- and four-digit numbers; in the fourth round, four- and five-digit numbers; in the fifth round, five- and six-digit numbers; in the sixth round, four- and five-digit numbers; in the seventh round, three- and four-digit numbers; in the eighth round, two- and three-digit numbers; and in the ninth and tenth rounds, one- and two-digit numbers.

The player with the most points after twenty rounds wins.

SAMPLE PLAY

Player A writes
<u>5</u> <u>17</u> <u>21</u> <u>8</u> <u>14</u> ......

Player B writes
<u>81</u> <u>49</u> <u>3</u> <u>34</u> <u>99</u> ......

The players trade lists.

A writes
$$\frac{81}{3} \quad \frac{49}{7} \quad \frac{3}{2} \quad \frac{34}{17} \quad \frac{99}{11} \quad ......$$

B writes
$$\frac{5}{7} \quad \frac{17}{34} \quad \frac{21}{7} \quad \frac{8}{16} \quad \frac{14}{4} \quad ......$$

The players trade lists again.

A calculates	B's points	B calculates	A's points
$\frac{5}{7} = 5 \div 7 = .7142857$	—10	$\frac{81}{3} = 81 \div 3 = 27$	27
$\frac{17}{34} = 17 \div 34 = .5$	—10	$\frac{49}{7} = 49 \div 7 = 7$	7
$\frac{21}{7} = 21 \div 7 = 3$	3	$\frac{3}{2} = 3 \div 2 = 1.5$	—10
$\frac{8}{16} = 8 \div 16 = .5$	—10	$\frac{34}{17} = 34 \div 17 = 2$	2
$\frac{14}{4} = 14 \div 4 = 3.5$	—10	$\frac{99}{11} = 99 \div 11 = 9$	9
and so on ...		and so on ...	

The game continues for ten rounds with the players writing three- and four-digit numbers in the next list of twenty numbers.

PASSING RATIOS

3 or More Players
1 Calculator per Player
Pencil and Paper
Watch

OBJECT OF THE GAME
To figure out a ratio within one minute.

THE PLAY
Each player writes down a two-digit number, no digits the same, and passes it to the player on the right. This player uses the number as a RESULT of a ratio, as a rational number. For example: Player A writes 10 and passes it to Player B. Player B must then figure out a ratio which results in 10 (100 ÷ 10 is a possibility). The players have one minute to come up with the ratio, and get one point.

The players then write down another rational number and pass it to the right. This time they increase the number of digits from 2 to 3, and continue to increase the digits every round. The digits must be different with each of the numbers.

The player with the most points after seven rounds is the winner.

SAMPLE PLAY

ROUND ONE

A writes 38
Passes it to B

B writes 14
Passes it to C

C writes 25
Passes it to A

(Players now try and find the ratio that would result in the number passed to them.)

A calculates that
$50 \div 2 = 25$
so ratio is 50/2

B calculates that
$2 \div 76 \neq 38$ but
$76 \div 2 = 38$
so ratio is 76/2

C calculates that
$7 \div 2 \neq 14$
$2 \div 28 \neq 14$
$28 \div 2 = 14$
so ratio is 28/2

does it in under a
minute and gets 1 point

does it in under a
minute so gets 1 point

does not do it in 1
minute so does not get
a point

ROUND TWO

A writes 450
Passes it to B

A calculates that
873 × 4 = 3492
3492 ÷ 4 = 873
so ratio is 3492/4

does not do it in
under a minute so gets
no point

B writes 241
Passes it to C

B calculates that
900 ÷ 2 = 450
so ratio is 900/2

does it in under a
minute and gets 1 point

C writes 873
Passes it to A

C calculates that
241 × 7 = 1687
1687 ÷ 7 = 241
so ratio is 1687/7

does it in under a
minute and gets 1 point

After Two Rounds....

A has 1 point

B has 2 points

C has 1 point

The game continues until seven rounds have been played. The player with the most points is the winner.

NOTE: ≠ means does not equal.

128

CHAPTER FIFTEEN: Power Play

Many mathematical ideas are shorthand ways to show something. For example: If you want to multiply $6 \times 6 \times 6 \times 6 = 1296$, you can write it this way: $6^4 = 1296$. "4" is the "power" or the "exponent" of 6 and means that 6 is multiplied by itself 4 times: $6 \times 6 \times 6 \times 6 = 6^4$. If you want to write 6 times itself 20 times, you would write 6^{20}.

One reason to make a number into a number and a power or exponent is to shorten the number. For example: $3,000,000,000$ can be written as 3×10^9 because $10^9 = 10 \times 10 \times 10 \times 10 \times 10 \times 10 \times 10 \times 10 \times 10 = 1,000,000,000 \times 3 = 3,000,000,000$. Some calculators have exponents in the readout on which you can enter 3×10^9.

The following numbers can be shortened with exponents in this way:

$6,000 = 6 \times 10^3$

$150,000 = 1.5 \times 10^5$

$7,986,000 = 7.986 \times 10^6$

$678,000,000,000 = 678 \times 10^9$

$275,000,000,000,000,000,000,000 = 275 \times 10^{21}$

$9,888,777,000,000,000,000,000,000,000,000,000,000 = 9,888,777 \times 10^{30}$

THE POWER HOUSE PUZZLE

To get from the Power Plant to the Power Houses, you must follow the Power Lines. Each of the Power Lines is a result of using a number between 1 and 9 as the base number and a number between 1 and 9 as the exponent number. For example: 3^2 means that 3 is the base number, and 2 is the exponent. To go from the Power Plant to the Power House, you must decide what the base number and the exponent number are for each number. Each Power Line is a series that goes from 1 to 9, or from 9 to 1 both in the base number or in the exponent number. For example: A Power Line that is not there might be 4, 16, 64, 256. . . . This would be 4^1, 4^2, 4^3, 4^4 since $4^1 = 4$, $4^2 = 16$, $4^3 = 64$, $4^4 = 256$. In the open spaces next to the Power Lines you can write the numbers and exponents if you like.

POWER HOUSE PUZZLE

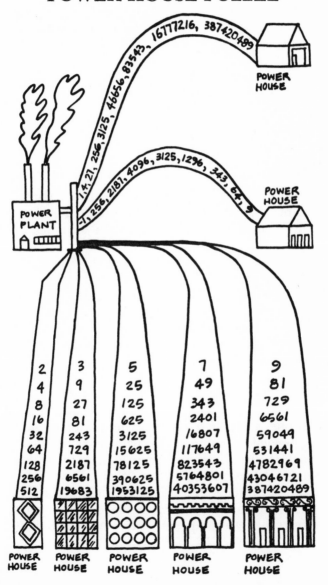

EXPO

2 Players
2 Calculators
Pencil and Paper
Watch

OBJECT OF THE GAME
To guess the highest exponent.

THE PLAY
Each player using his or her calculator figures out a number that can be made into more than one arrangement of number and exponent. For example: 16 can be 4^2 or 2^4. Each player writes down the number chosen and the number/exponent that it equals. For example, $64 = 2^6$. Both players then tell each other their numbers, BUT NOT THE NUMBER/EXPONENT. Each player tries to figure out the number/exponent combination which has the *largest* exponent. For example: If 16 was the number chosen, then 2^4 would have a larger exponent than 4^2. The players have two minutes to do this. After two minutes, the players reveal the number/exponent they have calculated. If it is the same as the original one, the player gets one point. If it is *lower,* the player whose number/exponent combination is being guessed gets a score equal to the difference between exponents. For example: If Player A used $16 = 2^4$, and Player B guesses $16 = 4^2$, Player A gets $4 - 2 = 2$ points. If the player guesses a higher exponent, the player guessing gets the difference. For example: If Player A used $16 = 4^2$ and Player B guesses $16 = 2^4$, Player B gets two points.

The game continues with the players making up new number/exponent combinations. The first player to get fifteen points wins the game.

SAMPLE PLAY

Player A writes 512
$512 = 2^9$

A says, "512"

In two minutes:
Player B calculates
$8 \times 8 \times 8 = 512 = 8^3$
B says, "8^3"
is wrong

So A gets $9 - 3 = 6$ points

B writes 4096
$4096 = 2^{12}$
B says, "4096"

A calculates
$4 \times 4 \times 4 \times 4 \times 4 \times 4 = 4096 = 4^6$
A says, "4^6"
is wrong

So B gets $12 - 6 = 6$ points

A writes 81
$81 = 3^4$
A says, "81"

B calculates
$3 \times 3 \times 3 \times 3 = 81 = 3^4$
B says, "3^4"
is right
So B gets 1 point

B writes 1024
$1024 = 4^5$
B says, "1024"

A calculates
$2 \times 2 \times 2 \times 2 \times 2 \times 2 \times 2 \times 2 \times 2 \times 2 = 1024 = 2^{10}$
A says, "2^{10}"
is wrong

but A has guessed a higher exponent
so gets $10 - 5 = 5$ points

and so on until one player accumulates fifteen points and wins.

NUMBER MAKER

3 or More Players
1 Calculator per Player
Pencil and Paper

OBJECT OF THE GAME

To guess the correct exponent of a number.

THE PLAY

The players take turns being Number Maker. The Number Maker makes up a number/exponent combination for every player, including himself. Then the Number Maker multiplies these number/exponent combinations and adds the result. (For example: $6^5 = 7776$, $4^2 = 16$, etc. and $7776 + 16 + $ etc. $= $)

Number Maker assigns one of these number/exponent combinations to each player, including himself, BUT TELLS THEM ONLY THE NUMBER, *NOT* THE EXPONENT. For example: For 6^5, Number Maker assigns 6 to a player. Then Number Maker tells all the players what the TOTAL is of all the number/exponent combinations added together. For example: If there are three players and three number/exponent combinations assigned: $4^5 + 6^5 + 8^4 = 1024 + 7776 + 4096 = 12896$ is the TOTAL that Number Maker announces.

Each player now must guess what exponent to use with the number assigned. For example: Player B is assigned 6, guesses that the exponent is 3, and tells that to Number Maker. If the player is correct, the player gets −10 points. If the player is wrong, the player gets the difference between the exponent he/she chose and the correct exponent TIMES 10. So, if a player guesses 6, and the correct exponent was 4, 6 − 4 = 2 × 10 = 20 points. Since the Number Maker knows the correct exponent automatically, Number Maker gets −10 points.

If all the players are wrong, then the Number Maker must multiply their number/exponent combinations, add them up and find the difference between that and the original total and divide it by 100. This will be the Number Maker's score (−10 which the Number Maker automatically gets). For example: The original Number Maker total is 12896. Player A guesses 4^6, Player B guesses 6^4, and Player C (Number Maker) knows 8^4. The total is 9488. So, 12896 − 9488 = 3408 ÷ 100 = 34.08. (Numbers should be rounded off to eliminate decimals.) The Number Maker gets a score of 34 − 10 = 24 points.

The player with the lowest score after ten rounds wins. If a player gets over 750 points, the player is out of the game.

To do well in this game requires that you calculate what the result of a number/exponent combination is, and remember that it is only one part of the total.

A new Number Maker is chosen after each round.

SAMPLE PLAY

Player A is Number Maker

chooses: $5^4 = 625$
$4^3 = 64$
$7^2 = 49$
$\overline{738}$

gives 5 to B
gives 4 to C
says, "738"

Number Maker
gets −10 points
automatically

B calculates
$5 \times 5 \times 5 \times 5 = 625 = 5^4$
says, "4"
is correct

B gets −10 points

C calculates
$4 \times 4 \times 4 = 64 = 4^3$
says, "3"
is correct

C gets −10 points

B is Number Maker
chooses: $9^2 = 81$
$6^3 = 216$
$4^6 = 4096$
$\overline{4393}$

gives 9 to A
gives 6 to C
says 4393

C calculates
$6 \times 6 \times 6 \times 6 = 1296 = 6^4$
says, "4"
is wrong
gets $4 - 3 = 1 \times 10 = 10$ points

A calculates
$9 \times 9 \times 9 = 729 = 9^3$
says, "3"
is wrong
gets $3 - 2 = 1 \times 10 = 10$ points

gets
```
    729
  +1296
   2025
   4393
  −2025
   2368
```

$2368 \div 100 = 23.68$
$= 24$
$24 - 10 = 14$ points

Total after A and B have been Number Makers

A has 10
−10
0 points

B has 14
−10
4 points

C has 10
−10
0 points

C is Number Maker
chooses: $10^3 = 1000$
$8^3 = 512$
$3^7 = 2187$
$\overline{3699}$

gives 10 to A
gives 3 to B
says, "3699"

gets $\begin{array}{r} 3699 \\ -243 \\ \hline 3456 \end{array}$

$3456 \div 100 = 34.56$
$= 35$

$35 - 10 = 25$ points

A calculates
$10 \times 10 \times 10 = 1000 = 10^3$
says, "3"
is right
gets -10 points

B calculates
$3 \times 3 \times 3 \times 3 \times 3 = 243 = 3^5$
says, "5"
is wrong
gets $7 - 5 = 2 \times 10 = 20$ points

Total after all players have been Number Makers

A has −10 points   B has 24 points   C has 25 points

and so on.

CHAPTER SIXTEEN:
Knowing Your Base

A base is a means of grouping things together. For example: Your fingers are grouped together by 10 since you have 10 fingers, and your toes are grouped together by 10, as well. But, you could say that your fingers are grouped by 5—5 fingers on your right hand and 5 on your left. A base is a grouping of things for the purpose of counting larger groups made up of smaller groups. When we can, we usually use a base group of 10. We count 1, 2, 3, 4, 5, 6, 7, 8, 9, 10 and then that is considered a group, and we add 10 to 1 and get 11 and 10 to 2 and get 12, and so on until the next group which starts with two (2 10's or 20). Our calculators are usually base grouped in 10's. After you count to 10, the first column is filled and the number goes to the second column.

Some things are base grouped by other numbers. For example: We count seconds on a base of 60. Once we count 60 seconds, we say that is 1 minute and then we count 60 more seconds and say that is 2 minutes and so on. The base group is a way to make it easier to handle large numbers. It would be pretty hard to say what time it is if we had only seconds to use. Nine o'clock in the morning would be 32400 o'clock! It is easier and faster to use seconds at base 60 and minutes at base 60 and say 9 o'clock.

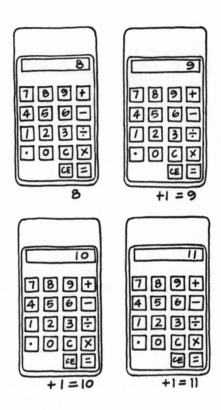

The puzzle below is the Base Course. Start on the lefthand side and go through the course. If you get stuck, consult the Base Chart, but try to do the course without using the chart.

BASE CHART

Seconds	= Base 60	Inches	= Base 12
Minutes	= Base 60	Feet	= Base 3
Hours	= Base 24	Yards	= Base 1760
Days	= Base 7	Millimeters	= Base 10
Weeks	= Base 52	Centimeters	= Base 10
		Decimeters	= Base 10
		Meters	= Base 1000

BASE COURSE

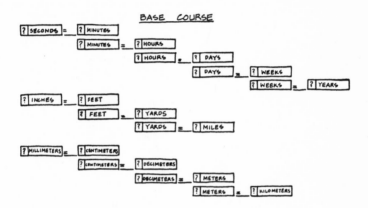

BASE COURSE

Now you are familiar with some bases and probably have discovered that there are many ways to base the same things. For example: Days can be based on 365 (365 = 1 year, or 7 days = 1 week). The following Base Maze can be figured out by doing the operation on the number in the box and then labeling what the base group is called.

For example:

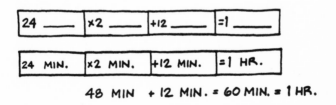

48 MIN + 12 MIN. = 60 MIN. = 1 HR.

Begin on the lefthand side of the maze and continue until you arrive at the box on the far right. Now, go to the next row and begin again. Each Base Maze line is a different set of base group units, e.g., seconds, minutes, or inches, feet, and so on.

BASE MAZE

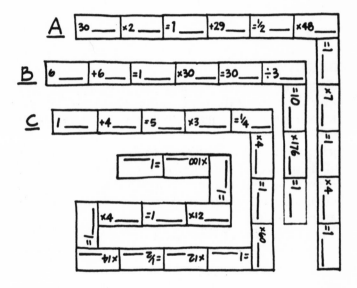

If the numbers are not working out, you are using the
wrong base group unit. Try another base group unit.

MAIN EVENT

2 Players
2 Calculators
Pencil and Paper
Watch

OBJECT OF THE GAME
To have the most points after ten rounds.

THE PLAY
Each player makes up a question to ask the other player concerning the composition of a large number. For example: "How many inches are there in 10,000 miles?" or "How many seconds are there in a year?" Each player figures out the answer to the question, and then asks the question of the other player. Both players have four minutes to figure out the answer to their opponent's question. A correct answer earns the player one point.

Players should double check their answers. If, by chance, the player who invented the question has the wrong answer, that player gets a −1 point.

The game continues for ten rounds of questions. The winner is the player with the most points after ten rounds.

Suggestions for Questions
   How many hours are there in ten years?
   How many ounces are there in one million tons?
   How many seconds have you been alive?
   How many seconds have passed since the signing of
      the Constitution?

More about Bases:

Counting in different bases is difficult. If we are counting in Base 10 and then shift to Base 5, it is like changing languages and trying to say the same thing. For example: If we see the word "sale," we think that it means the store is selling something at a lower price, but in French the word "sale" means dirty. So although the word looks the same it means something very different. If we see the number 44 it means there are 44 things BUT ONLY IN BASE 10. In Base 5, 44 means *there are 24 things!* The following discussion will explain this fully.

Counting in Base 5, you count 1, 2, 3, 4, and then you would write 10 which equals 5 in Base 5. In Base 10, you count 1, 2, 3, 4, 5, 6, 7, 8, 9, and then write 10. In Base 5, you count 1, 2, 3, 4, and then write 10 because there now is one group of 5. If you continue to count in Base 5, you would write 6 as 11, 7 as 12, 8 as 13, 9 as 14, and 10 as 20.

In Base 5 you have the same kind of hidden multipliers as in Base 10. So, in the first column of a number, you would multiply by 1, the second column by 5, the third column by 25, the fourth column by 125, the fifth column by 625 (going from left to right, 5^4, 5^3, 5^2, 5^1). This is the same as in Base 10 where you multiply the first column by 1, the second by 10, the third by 100, the fourth by 1000, and the fifth by 10,000.

Here is a comparison between numbers in Base 10 and numbers in Base 5:

BASE 10	BASE 5
1	1
2	2
3	3
4	4
5	10
6	11

BASE 10	BASE 5
7	12
8	13
9	14
10	20
24	44
25	50
35	120
50	200
75	300
125	1000

Each time you make a new base, the way of writing the numbers will change. When you change from Base 10 to another base, first look to see how many of the largest *powers* of that base fit into the numbers. For example: with 75, you can see that the largest power of 5 in 75 is $5^2 = 25$, of which there are three in 75. There are three 25's in 75, no 5's and no 1's. So, 75 would be written as 300 in Base 5.

How would you write 81? There are three 25's, one 5, and one 1. So it would be 311.

See how the base 10 numbers change into other base numbers below.

BASE 10	BASE 2	BASE 3	BASE 4	BASE 5	BASE 6
1	1	1	1	1	1
2	10	2	2	2	2
3	11	10	3	3	3
4	100	11	10	4	4
5	101	12	11	10	5
6	110	20	12	11	10
25	11001	221	121	100	41
64	100000	2101	1000	224	144

Before you play Base Runner, practice switching bases.

BASE RUNNER

3 or More Players
1 Calculator per Player

OBJECT OF THE GAME

To have the most points after each player has been the Base Runner three times.

THE PLAY

Each player selects a base by which to play. In other words, a player could select Base 6, or Base 10, or Base 5, etc. The player must keep this Base for the entire game *unless* it is guessed by the Base Runner.

Player A is the first Base Runner. Base Runner A says any two-digit number and an operation ($+$, $-$, $\times$, $\div$), and another, different two-digit number. (For example: $20 + 55$.) The other players put this into their calculators, do the operation, and then divide the result by the highest power of their Base. For example: Player B has chosen Base 5, so $20 + 55 = 75$, and then divides 75 by the highest power of Base 5. The highest power of Base 5 is 25. There are three 25's. So Player B writes 75 in Base 5 as 300. After this is done, the Base Runner asks each player for the result (Player B would say 300), and then the Base Runner has to guess the player's base.

If the Base Runner guesses correctly, he/she gets one point. After the Base Runner makes his/her guesses, another player becomes the Base Runner.

The game continues until all players have been the Base Runner three times. The player with the most points wins.

SAMPLE PLAY

A	**B**	**C**
A is Base Runner	selects Base 6	selects Base 5
says, "20 $\times$ 15"	20 $\times$ 15 = 300	20 $\times$ 15 = 300
	6^3 = 216	5^3 = 125
	300 — 216 = 84	125 $\times$ 2 = 250
	6^2 = 36	300 — 250 = 50
	36 $\times$ 2 = 72	5^2 = 25
	84 — 72 = 12	25 $\times$ 2 = 50
	6 $\times$ 2 = 12	50 — 50 = 0

Base Runner asks for results

B says, "1220"   C says, "2200"

Base Runner guesses

B used Base 4
is wrong, gets 0 points.

Base Runner guesses

C used Base 5
is right, gets 1 point.

And the play continues.

CHAPTER SEVENTEEN:
Hundred Percent

Percents represent parts of another number, like fractions or decimal numbers. For example: 25 percent of 40 = 10 which means that ¼ of 40 = 10. Think of 40 divided into 4 parts (quarters, ¼'s) and each part is 10, 10 + 10 + 10 + 10 = 40. If you change ¼ into its decimal equivalent, it is .25 (.25 × 40 = 10). This says that 25 percent of 40 is 10. But you write 25 percent as .25. Why? Because 25 percent is equal to ¼ and ¼ is equal to .25.

When you see a number and percentage sign, like 25 percent, you can convert it to a decimal. 25 percent = .25. If you want to know what 25 percent of a number is, multiply the number by .25. What if you want 5 percent of a number? Multiply the number by .05. What about 2½ percent of a number? Multiply the number by .025. What about 102½ percent of a number? Multiply the number by 1.025.

THE PERCENT MAZE

To do the Percent Maze, you will need your calculator and pencil and paper. The object of this maze is to get from Start to Finish as fast as you can.

Begin at Start. Figure out the percentage in the box, do the operation that follows, figure out the next percentage, and do the next operation, and so on until you get to Finish.

For example: 46 percent of 2000 is __?__ . Then subtract 125 percent of 125 from that, and so on. Write down your results as you move along so you can check yourself if you get stuck.

PERCENT MAZE

START

0 + | 46% of 2000 | — | 125 % of 125 | + | 3% of 4326 |

| 59% of 5963 | +←

| 66⅔% of 1000 | + | 96% of 4598 | — | 59% of 5963 |

↳ + | 40% of 4000 | — | 65% of 1000 | — | 1000% of 85 |

| 1% of 4268 | +←

| 2½% of 6542 | — | 16% of 2814 | + | 1% of 4268 |

↳ — | 6% of 6821 | + | 37% of 1895 | + | 116% of 321 |

| 55% of 5555 | +←

| 75% of 6543 | + | 50% of 7500 | — | 55% of 5555 |

↳ + | 25% of 5879 | — | 81% of 8100 | — | 1% of 87849 |

= ↓ 0

FINISH

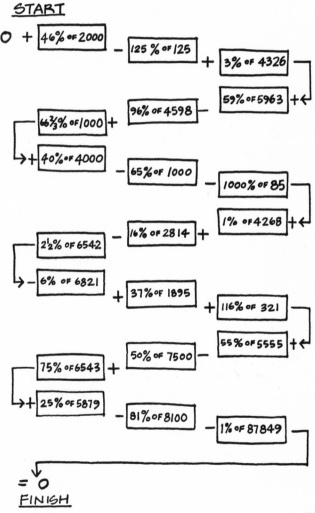

PLAYING PERCENTAGES

2 Players
2 Calculators
Pencil and Paper

OBJECT OF THE GAME

For both players to have their numbers within fifty points of each other after trading percentages ten times (five trades per player).

THE PLAY

Each player enters a six-digit number in his or her calculator, no digits the same. The players do not show their numbers to each other. Player A asks for a percentage between 0 and 9 of Player B's number; for example: "Give me 6 percent of your number." Player B calculates what 6 percent of his/her number is and gives it to Player A, who adds it to his/her number while B subtracts it from his/her number.

Now Player B asks Player A for a percentage of A's number. Player A calculates the percentage of the number A now has in his/her calculator. For example: Player A had 654321 as A's original number. Player B gives A 567.6 as the percentage requested, so A adds 654321 + 567.6 = 654888.6. Player A now figures the percentage requested by B of new number 654888.6, NOT 654321.

The players trade percentages ten times (five trades per player) and then compare numbers. If they are within fifty points, they have succeeded. If not, they play again.

SAMPLE PLAY

A enters 987654
writes 987654

A says, "Give me 20% of your number"

987654 + 24936 = 1012590

A calculates
1012590 × .05 = 50629.5
says, "50629.5"

1012590 − 50629.5 = 961960.5

A says, "Give me ½% of your number"

961960.5 + 751.8675 = 962712.36

B enters 124680
writes 124680

B calculates
124680 × .2 = 24936
says, "24936"
124680 − 24936 = 99744

B says, "Give me 5% of your number"

99744 + 50629.5 = 150373.5

B calculates
150373.5 × .005 = 751.8675
says, "751.8675"
150373.5 − 751.8675 = 149621.64

B says, "Give me 50% of your number"

A calculates
962712.36 × .5 = 481356.18
says, "481356.18"

962712.36 − 481356.18 = 481356.18

A says, "Give me 15% of your number"

481356.18 + 94646.673 = 576002.85

A calculates
576002.85 × .08 = 46080.228
says, "46080.228"

576002.85 − 46080.228 = 529922.63

A says, "Give me 3% of your number"

149621.64 + 481356.18 = 630977.82

B calculates
630977.82 × .15 = 94646.673
says, "94646.673"

630977.82 − 94646.673 = 536331.15

B says, "Give me 8% of your number"

536331.15 + 46080.228 = 582411.37

B calculates
582411.37 × .03 = 17472.341
says, "17472.341"

529922.63 + 17472.341 = 547394.97

A calculates
547394.97 × .02 = 10947.899
says, "10947.899"

547394.97 − 10947.899 = 536447.08

A says, "Give me ¼% of your number"

536447.08 + 1439.7173 = 537886.79

A calculates
537886.79 × .00125 = 672.35848
says, "672.35848"

537886.79 − 672.35848 = 537214.44

582411.37 − 17472.341 = 564939.03

B says, "Give me 2% of your number"

564939.03 + 10947.899 = 575886.92

B calculates
575886.92 × .0025 = 1439.7173
says, "1439.7173"

575886.92 − 1439.7173 = 574447.21

B says, "Give me ⅛% of your number"

574447.21 + 672.35848 = 575119.56

At this point, the two players find the difference between their numbers

$$575119.56 - 537214.44 = 37905.12$$

The players did not get their numbers within 50, so they will start another game by entering new six-digit numbers.

BANKROLL

3 or More Players
1 Calculator per Player
Dice

OBJECT OF THE GAME

To have the highest number after one (or two) round(s) of trading percentages.

THE PLAY

Each player enters a four-digit number in his/her calculator, no digits the same. This is the player's Bankroll. Each player then figures out the highest percentage of his/her Bankroll that he or she can lose and still keep $100. For example: If Player A has

$4321, then Player A can lose 97 percent and still retain $100.

Each player rolls the dice to see who goes first. Highest roll goes first, second highest second, and so forth. Player A rolls the dice. The number that appears is the percentage of the Bankroll that Player A must give away to Player B. Player A calculates the percentage in terms of his/her dollars and gives it to Player B who writes it down. Player A rolls the dice again and gives away that percentage of A's *original* Bankroll to Player C, and so on until A has given a percentage to every player.

Then it is B's turn. Player B follows the same procedure. When all the players have given away percentages of their Bankroll to all the other players, and the players have written these percentages down (without adding them to their Bankroll), each player decides whether he/she wants to play another round.

If they decide to play another round, they follow the same procedure. If they do not play another round, the players can *either* use what remains of their Bankroll, OR they can use the total of the amounts given to each of them by the other players.

Each player must decide whether what he/she has is the highest he/she will get, or whether he/she should chance another round hoping to add to the written total and to win the game with the highest Bankroll.

If a player decides not to play another round, the player does not risk anything, even if the other players decide to play another round. The other players trade with each other. When the second round is over, ALL players compare Bankrolls. If any player has less than 100 in his/her calculator, the player automatically loses. The player with the highest Bankroll either on his/her calculator or in the total of amounts given to him/her by other players, wins. EACH GAME MAY NOT CONTINUE AFTER TWO ROUNDS. PLAYERS MAY START A NEW GAME IF THEY WISH.

SAMPLE PLAY

A	B	C
A enters 1234 as Bankroll	B enters 9753 as Bankroll	C enters 2468 as Bankroll
figures can lose 91% of number without going under 100	figures can lose 98% of number without going under 100	figures can lose 95% of number without going under 100
rolls dice	rolls dice	rolls dice
gets 6	gets 7	gets 12
A goes third	B goes second	C goes first
		rolls dice
		gets 10
		must give 10% to B
		$2468 \times .1 = 246.8$
		$2468 - 246.8 = 2221.2$
	writes 246.8	
		rolls dice
		gets 4
		must give 4% to A
		$2468 \times .04 = 98.72$
		$2221.2 - 98.72 = 2122.48$
writes 98.72		

B rolls dice
gets 8
must give 8% to A

$9753 \times .08 = 780.24$
$9753 - 780.24 = 8972.76$

writes 780.24

rolls dice
gets 6
must give 6% to C

$9753 \times .06 = 585.18$
$8972.76 - 585.18 = 8387.58$

writes 585.18

A rolls dice
gets 9
must give 9% to C

$1234 \times .09 = 111.06$
$1234 - 111.06 = 1122.94$

rolls dice
gets 8
must give 8% to B

writes 111.06

1284 × .08 = 98.72
1122.94 − 98.72 = 1024.22

writes 98.72

Remaining Bankroll
1024.22   8387.58   2122.48

Total of Written Numbers
98.72 + 780.24 = 878.96   246.8 + 98.72 = 345.52   585.18 + 111.06 = 696.24

A decides that since neither Remaining Bankroll nor Total of Written Numbers is high enough, will play another round.

B decides that Remaining Bankroll will win the game, so steps out of playing until the end of the game.

C decides that since neither Remaining Bankroll nor Total of Written Numbers is high enough, will play another round.

A

C
goes first
rolls dice
gets 11
must give 11% to A
2468 × .11 = 271.48
2122.48 − 271.48 = 1851

writes 271.48

rolls dice
gets 6
must give 6% to C

$1234 \times .06 = 74.04$
$1024.22 - 74.04 = 950.18$

writes 74.04

The game has ended. All the players compare numbers.

Remaining Bankroll
950.18   8387.58   1851

Total of Written Numbers:
$878.96 + 271.48$
$= 1150.44$ 345.52 $696.24 + 74.04 = 770.28$

B wins the game with 8387.58

CHAPTER EIGHTEEN:
Prime Time

Certain numbers can be divided evenly only by themselves and 1. For example: 7 can be evenly divided by 7, and it can be evenly divided by 1. Try it. But if 7 is divided by any other whole number, the result will have a decimal part. For example: $7 \div 6 = 1.1666$ or $7 \div 5 = 1.4$ etc.

One can be evenly divided only by itself. Two can be evenly divided only by itself and 1. Three can be evenly divided by itself and 1, and so on. Numbers that can be evenly divided by themselves and 1 are called Prime Numbers.

THE PRIME PUZZLE

Find all the Prime Numbers in this puzzle.

```
 1  2   3   4   5   6   7   8   9  10  11  12  13  14  15  16  17  18  19 20
21 22  23  24  25  26  27  28  29  30  31  32  33  34 35
36 37  38  39  40  41  42  43  44  45  46  47  48  49  50  51
52 53  54  55  56  57  58  59  60  61  62  63  64  65  66  67
68 69  70  71  72  73  74  75  76  77  78  79  80  81  82
83 84  85  86  87  88  89  90  91  92  93  94  95  96  97
98 99 100
```

In the Appendix, you'll find a list of all the Prime Numbers between 1 and 1000. Check your results against that list.

PRIME GAME

2 Players
2 Calculators
Pencil and Paper

OBJECT OF THE GAME

To find all the Prime Numbers in the Prime Box within twenty minutes, working with the other player.

THE PLAY

The Prime Box has numbers in it that are Prime Numbers and many that are not. Working with another player, figure out which numbers are Prime and which are not. Give yourself a twenty-minute time limit to make the game exciting. When you figure out the Prime Numbers, circle them, and the squares will fall into a pattern of two words which will tell you what you are. . . . Since you are working together with someone else, when you succeed you are both what the words say.

PRIME BOX

130	404	215	393	458	198	477	352	208	361	392	476	282
305	427	475	104	333	489	102	459	372	426	132	406	508
162	244	522	334	441	416	275	496	284	456	351	488	234
404	445	359	617	457	206	293	661	281	466	373	214	419
207	320	509	265	367	370	569	507	307	236	563	190	557
174	425	127	409	571	128	131	733	311	318	139	124	149
394	415	199	187	473	264	197	253	251	369	191	302	701
106	343	257	403	111	402	449	553	521	205	613	315	431
230	368	474	110	424	200	483	148	423	285	387	155	532
154	360	101	313	577	460	401	221	587	531	107	797	593
306	442	157	288	414	321	163	358	673	388	173	530	787
143	342	263	493	164	506	103	211	269	287	271	727	331
289	444	461	329	462	341	631	322	317	435	541	300	757
386	493	619	223	397	505	523	436	683	220	443	545	337
201	245	385	472	526	356	384	527	202	464	365	546	122
380	524	144	492	119	445	504	185	528	355	118	446	561
209	395	328	525	186	418	267	396	327	529	168	301	554

498	102	520	304	490	242	440	362	455	519	176	552
417	266	486	407	136	468	537	147	551	378	568	325
510	391	303	371	497	350	485	550	429	252	454	501
677	379	761	421	535	277	547	743	438	500	408	428
314	739	150	659	213	691	192	194	517	112	560	410
120	181	534	773	536	151	607	538	345	496	114	566
172	233	376	719	332	193	578	559	175	539	224	248
484	503	511	463	548	491	353	653	324	390	548	437
336	274	533	375	212	549	204	453	452	567	160	363
465	109	229	433	439	383	303	227	643	467	348	452
210	167	422	769	482	751	402	179	565	601	564	272
366	599	481	283	357	389	291	113	647	479	542	308
323	239	153	709	414	487	515	241	290	516	142	411
434	641	512	347	570	499	292	349	572	374	558	226
471	286	513	447	203	544	247	573	430	246	412	470
312	502	116	555	413	543	480	448	346	450	574	310
354	478	268	364	556	138	514	326	575	180	562	273

HEAVY HAND

3 or More Players
1 Calculator per Player
Pencil and Paper
Watch

OBJECT OF THE GAME

To find the Prime Numbers in your Prime Hand and get ten points before the other players.

THE PLAY

Each player enters a five-digit number, no digits the same, presses the divide button, enters another five-digit number, no digits the same, and presses the equal key. The result, whole and decimal numbers, is the player's Prime Hand.

Each player has sixty seconds to study his/her hand and find the Prime Numbers in it. For example: If a player's hand is .3452679, 3, 5, 2, 67, 79 are Primes (THE PRIMES MUST APPEAR ADJACENT IN THE PRIME HAND, so although 47 is a Prime, it can't be used since 4 is not adjacent to 7). If a player can use all the numbers in the hand to make Prime Numbers, the player gets an extra point.

Once the players have discovered their Primes, they tell the others the results. The player with the most Primes wins the hand and gets one point. If tied, each player gets one point.

The Prime Numbers can be one-, two-, three-digit numbers. The players should write down their Prime Hand and then use the calculator to check if a number is Prime.

To make the game exciting, keep the rounds short so that the players must guess fast and accurately. If a player says that he/she has a certain number of Primes, and is wrong, the player gets minus one point.

The first player to get ten points wins.

SAMPLE PLAY

A enters 46823	B enters 12345	C enters 98752
46823 ÷ 12345 = 3.7928716	12345 ÷ 87654 = .1408378	98752 ÷ 21067 = 4.6875207
A says that	B says that	C says that
3 is prime	1 is prime	7 is prime
37 is prime	83 is prime	207 is prime
79 is prime	37 is prime	87 is prime
379 is prime		
287 is prime		
87 is prime		
871 is prime		
71 is prime		

A checks guesses	B checks guesses and is right	C checks guesses
finds that		finds that
$287 \div 7 = 41$		$207 \div 3 = 69$
$87 \div 3 = 29$		$87 \div 3 = 29$
gets —1 point	gets 1 point	gets —1 point

The game continues with the players finding new Prime Hands and guessing the Prime Numbers in their hands.

CHAPTER NINETEEN:
Easy Conversion

To measure something we make up a definite standard length, or standard weight, or number and then compare it with what we want to measure. For example: If we use the standard length of an inch, we use a ruler which is marked by inches, to see how many inches are contained along the length of an object we want to measure. If we have an ounce weight, then we weigh it against the object we are weighing to see how many ounces of weight will balance the scale against the object being weighed.

Different countries and peoples use different standards of measurement. In the last fifty years two standards have emerged as the most popular—the English and the Metric. The English System which is used in the United States and England is based on inches/feet/yards/miles for distance, liquid ounces/pints/quarts/gallons for liquid measure, and ounces/pounds/tons for weight measure. The Metric System is based on meters and sub-units and multiple units for distance/ liters and sub-units and multiple units for liquid measure, and grams and sub-units and multiple units for weight measure. The difference between the two systems is simply the difference of a base unit (see Base Chapter). Consult the charts below to see how the units are converted.

CONVERSION FACTORS

Conversion Factors—Metric to English

TO OBTAIN	MULTIPLY	BY
Inches	Centimeters	0.3937007874
Feet	Meters	3.280839895
Yards	Meters	1.093613298
Miles	Kilometers	0.6213711922
Ounces	Grams	$3.527396195 \times 10^{-2}$
Pounds	Kilograms	2.204622622
Gallons	Liters	0.2641720524
Fluid ounces	Milliliters (cc)	$3.381402270 \times 10^{-2}$
Square inches	Square centimeters	0.1550003100
Square feet	Square meters	10.76391042
Square yards	Square meters	1.195990046
Cubic inches	Milliliters (cc)	$6.102374409 \times 10^{-2}$
Cubic feet	Cubic meters	35.31466672
Cubic yards	Cubic meters	1.307950619

Conversion Factors—English to Metric

TO OBTAIN	MULTIPLY	BY
Centimeters	Inches	2.54
Meters	Feet	0.3048
Meters	Yards	0.9144
Kilometers	Miles	1.609344
Grams	Ounces	28.34952313
Kilograms	Pounds	0.45359237
Liters	Gallons	3.785411784
Milliliters (cc)	Fluid ounces	29.57352956
Square centimeters	Square inches	6.4516
Square meters	Square feet	0.09290304
Square meters	Square yards	0.83612736
Milliliters (cc)	Cubic inches	16.387064
Cubic meters	Cubic feet	$2.831684659 \times 10^{-2}$
Cubic meters	Cubic yards	0.764554858

(It will be difficult to use decimals with more than three decimal places, so to proceed with the puzzle, round off decimals to three places. For example: .45359237 should be rounded off to .454; and .9144 should be rounded off to .914.)

THE CONVERSION MAZE

In this puzzle, you must convert measurement through the systems of Metric to English to Metric. Begin with 800 inches and find out how many centimeters that equals, then how many feet, and so on. Fill in each question mark with the correct number.

1. 800 INCHES = (   )? CENTIMETERS = (   )? FEET = (   )? METERS = (   )? YARDS = (   )? METERS = (   )? MILES = (   )? KILOMETERS

2. 750 OUNCES = (   )? GRAMS = (   )? POUNDS = (   )? KILOGRAMS = (   )? KILOGRAMS = (   )? TONS   (THERE ARE 2000 POUNDS IN A TON)

3. 185 LIQUID OUNCES = (   )? PINTS = (   )? QUARTS = (   )? GALLONS = (   )? LITERS = (   )? MILLILITERS

4. 6000 SQUARE INCHES = (   )? SQUARE CENTIMETERS = (   )? SQUARE FEET = (   )? SQUARE METERS = (   )? SQUARE YARDS = (   )? SQUARE METERES = (   )? SQUARE MILES = (   )? SQUARE KILOMETERS

5. 2400 CUBIC INCHES = (   )? CUBIC CENTIMETERS = (   )? CUBIC FEET = (   )? CUBIC METERS = (   )? CUBIC YARDS = (   )? CUBIC METERS = (   )? CUBIC MILES = (   )? CUBIC KILOMETERS

QUICK CONVERSION

2 Players
2 Calculators
Pencil and Paper

OBJECT OF THE GAME

To guess the conversion factor.

THE PLAY

Each player selects one set of conversion factors; for example: inches to centimeters, or centimeters to inches. Then each player enters a three-digit number in his/her calculator and converts it from one of the units to the other. The players write down the first three-digit number and the number to which it is converted, BUT NOT THE CONVERSION UNIT. For example: If a player chooses 100 inches = 254 centimeters, then the player writes down 100 and 254.

Players now exchange pieces of paper, and each player has sixty seconds to guess the correct conversion fact used. If the player is correct, the player gets one point. If the player is wrong, the player gets no points. After sixty seconds the player must stop.

The game continues with each player selecting a new three-digit number and converting it. The play continues for ten rounds. The player with the most points after ten rounds wins.

SAMPLE PLAY

A selects yards to meters	B selects grams to ounces
enters 450	enters 120
converts	converts
$450 \times 1.09 = 490.5$	$120 \times 28.4 = 3408$
writes 450 490.5 and passes to B	writes 120 3408 and passes to A
Within 1 minute A guesses B's conversion by calculating	Within 1 minute B guesses A's conversion by calculating
$3408 \div 120 = 28.4$	$490.5 \div 450 = 1.09$
Consults chart A guesses that B has converted grams to ounces	Consults chart B guesses that A has converted yards to meters
A is right	B is right
A gets 1 point	B gets 1 point

The play continues with each player entering a new three-digit number and converting it. The player with the most points after ten rounds wins the game.

HIGH NO/LOW NO

3 or More Players
1 Calculator per Player

OBJECT OF THE GAME

To avoid having the highest or lowest number in a round.

THE PLAY

Each player enters a five-digit number, no digits the same, presses the divide button, enters another five-digit number, and presses the equal button. The first four digits to the right of the decimal point are the player's UNIT NUMBER. Each player now consults the Conversion Factor Chart and decides what units the UNIT NUMBER is going to be in. For example: A player has 1234 as his/her Unit Number and selects inches as the unit.

Each player now says out loud the Lead Digit of his/her Unit Number. For example: In Unit Number 1234, 1 is the Lead Digit. The players listen to the other players' Lead Digits and decide whether or not to convert their Unit Number to another unit. For example: The Player with 1234 might think this number is too low and convert it to centimeters: $1234 \times 2.54 = 3134.36$. The players are trying to avoid having the highest or lowest number in the group. A player may make only one conversion. Then all players show their numbers. The players with the lowest and highest number get minus one point. The other players get one point.

The game continues for fifteen rounds. The player with the highest score wins.

SAMPLE PLAY

A	B	C	D
A enters $12345 \div 78963 = .156339$	B enters $98765 \div 12345 = 8.000405$	C enters $43587 \div 67890 = .6420238$	D enters $24689 \div 35910 = .6875243$
1563 is A's Unit Number	0004 is B's Unit Number	6420 is C's Unit Number	6875 is D's Unit Number
selects feet	selects grams	selects miles	selects meters
A says 1 is Lead Digit	B says 0 is Lead Digit	C says 6 is Lead Digit	D says 6 is Lead Digit
decides not to convert	decides to convert to ounces	decides to convert to kilometers	decides to convert to feet
calculator reads 1563	$0004 \times 28.4 = 113.6$	$6420 \times .621 = 3986.82$	$6875 \times .305 = 2096.875$
A wins gets 1 point	B gets −1 point	C gets −1 point	D wins gets 1 point

The play continues with the players finding new Unit Numbers and selecting new units. After fifteen rounds, the player with the highest number of points wins the game.

CHAPTER TWENTY:
Making Both
Sides Equal

When you go for a walk to a certain place you make a map in your mind so that you can get there. You might think, "Turn right at the first corner, walk two blocks, turn left, and I'm there." There are probably several ways to get to the same place. When you do a series of operations with numbers, there are also often several ways to get to the same place. For example: If your destination is 25, you can do:

$$(1) \ 3 + 4 + 5 + 10 + 3 = 25$$
$$(2) \ 5 \times 5 = 25$$
$$(3) \ (4 \times 4) + (3 \times 3) = 25 \ \text{etc.}$$

These are different routes to the same number, and they are equal to each other since they are equal to the same number, 25. These are equations.

EQUATIONS MARATHON

The object of the Equations Marathon is to get to the central number in each star by adding, subtracting, multiplying, or dividing in the assigned number of ways. The samples at the bottom of the Equations Marathon give you an idea of one of the routes for each star. Use at least two numbers for each equation and use all the operations (+, −, ×, ÷) at least once in each star.

> 560 in 10 ways
> 1050 in 12 ways
> 122 in 7 ways
> 888 in 6 ways
> 3000 in 12 ways

EQUATIONS MARATHON

Equations sometimes have one or more missing elements. For example: You might forget one of the directions for getting someplace. You know that you have to turn right at the second corner, but you have forgotten how many blocks you then have to walk before making a left turn. This can happen with numbers, too. For example: You have the following equation:

EQUATIONS MARATHON

SAMPLE
56 × 10 = 560
10 × 100 = 1000 + 50 = 1050
12 × 12 = 144 − 22 = 122
8 × 11 = 88 + 800 = 888
60 × 50 = 3000

$$(34 + 4 + X) \times 2 = 80$$

How can you find out what X equals? First, add the numbers within the parentheses: $34 + 4 = 38$, and then there is X. Now, multiply $38 \times 2 = 76$, and multiply $X \times 2 = 2X$. The equation now looks like this: $76 + 2X = 80$. Since an equation means that one side equals the other side, you can keep them that way if you do the same operation to both sides. You can subtract 76 from both sides: $76 + 2X - 76 = 80 - 76$. This leaves $2X = 4$. Now, divide both sides by 2: $2X \div 2 = 4 \div 2$; therefore, $X = 2$. Go back to the original equation and put 2 where X was: $(34 + 4 + 2) \times 2 = 80, 80 = 80$.

EQUATION GAME

2 Players
2 Calculators
Pencil and Paper

OBJECT OF THE GAME
To find out "what X equals" first.

THE PLAY
Each player writes an Equation with at least three numbers and one X. For example: $(34 + X + 4) \times 2 = 80$.

The players each calculate what X equals and write it down on a separate piece of paper. Now, the players exchange their equations. The players try to solve "what X equals" before the other player does. The first player to do so says, "I got it." Then both players pass back the equations. If the player is correct, he/she gets one point. If the player is wrong, the player who made up the equation gets one point. If the player is wrong and does not say, "I got it," the originator of the equation gets one point.

Play continues for eleven rounds. The player with the most points at the end of eleven rounds is the winner.

SAMPLE PLAY

A writes $4 \times (8 \times X - 7) = 100$ and passes to B

B writes $8 + 5X + 13 = 76$ and passes to A

A calculates B's equation

$$8 + 5X + 13 = 76$$
$$21 + 5X = 76$$

$$21 + 5X - 21 = 76 - 21$$
$$5X = 55$$
$$X = 11$$

Says, "I got it!" first

B calculates A's equation

$$4 \times (8 \times X - 7) = 100$$
$$32X - 28 = 100$$

$$32X - 28 + 28 = 100 + 28$$
$$32X = 128$$
$$X = 4$$

A passes answer back to B to check it

$$8 + 5 \times (11) + 13 = 76$$
$$8 + 55 + 13 = 76$$

A has gotten the answer right, so A gets 1 point

B passes answer back to A to check it

$$4 \times (8 \times 4 - 7) = 100$$
$$4 \times (32 - 7) = 100$$
$$4 \times (25) = 100$$

B has gotten the right answer but did not say, "I got it!" first, so B gets no points.

X

3 or More Players
1 Calculator per Player
Pencils and Paper

OBJECT OF THE GAME
To be the first to figure out what X equals.

THE PLAY
Each player writes an equation with at least three operations and with all numbers using X. For example: $(6 \times X) + (5 + X) - (3 - X) + (20 \div X) = 28$. X must be the same number in each of the parentheses. Then the player figures out the answer. For example: in the above equation, $X = 2$. The player writes the equation and the answer without showing what X is.

Each player is passed an equation and has three minutes to solve it. After three minutes, the players return the equations to their owners. If it is right, the player gets one point. If it is wrong, the player who wrote the equation gets one point.

Play continues for fifteen rounds and the player with the most points after fifteen rounds is the winner.

The players should make the equations more complicated and use larger numbers each round.

SAMPLE PLAY

A writes $(3 \times X) + (X - 5) - (4 + 2 \times X) - (X - 4) = 5$
and passes to B

B writes $(X + 2) + (7 \times X) - (19 + X) + (3 \times X + 1) = 74$
and passes to C

C writes $(25 + X) - (4 \times X) + (9 - X) + (X) = 25$
and passes to A

In three minutes

A calculates C's equation
$$25 + X - (4 \times X) + 9 - X + X = 25$$
$$34 - 3X = 25$$
$$34 - 3X - 34 = 25 - 34$$
$$-3X = -9$$
$$X = 3$$

A passes answer back to C to check it
$$(25 + 3) - (4 \times 3) + (9 - 3) + (3) = 25$$
$$28 - 12 + 6 + 3 = 25$$

A is right so gets 1 point

In three minutes

B calculates A's equation
$$(3 \times X) + X - 5 - 4 - (2 \times X) - X + 4 = 5$$
$$X - 5 = 5$$
$$X - 5 + 5 = 5 + 5$$
$$X = 10$$

B passes answer back to A to check it
$$(3 \times 10) + (10 - 5) - (4 + 20) - (10 - 4) = 5$$
$$30 + 5 - 24 - 6 = 5$$

B is right so gets 1 point

In three minutes

C calculates B's equation
$$X + 2 + (7 \times X) - 19 - X + 3X + 1 = 74$$
$$10X - 16 = 74$$
$$10X - 16 + 16 = 74 + 16$$
$$10X = 90$$
$$X = 9$$

C passes answer back to B to check it
$$(9 + 2) + (7 \times 9) - (19 + 9) + (27 + 1) = 74$$
$$11 + 63 - 28 + 28 = 74$$

C is right so gets 1 point

The play continues for fifteen rounds. The player with the most points after fifteen rounds wins the game.

Appendix

Prime Numbers between 1 and 1000

1	113	281	463	659	863
2	127	283	467	661	877
3	131	293	479	673	881
5	137	307	487	677	883
7	139	311	491	683	887
11	149	313	499	691	907
13	151	317	503	701	911
17	157	331	509	709	919
19	163	337	521	719	929
23	167	347	523	727	937
29	173	349	541	733	941
31	179	353	547	739	947
37	181	359	557	743	953
41	191	367	563	751	967
43	193	373	569	757	971
47	197	379	571	761	977
53	199	383	577	769	983
59	211	389	587	773	991
61	223	397	593	787	997
67	227	401	599	797	
71	229	409	601	809	
73	233	419	607	811	
79	239	421	613	821	
83	241	431	617	823	
89	251	433	619	827	
97	257	439	631	829	
101	263	443	641	839	
103	269	449	643	853	
107	271	457	647	857	
109	277	461	653	859	

The Authors

Edwin Schlossberg received Ph.D. degrees in Science and Literature from Columbia University. He has taught at Columbia University, M.I.T., and the University of Illinois, and designed the Learning Environment for the Brooklyn Children's Museum. He is the author of *Wordswordswords, Einstein and Beckett* and coauthor of *Projex*. Dr. Schlossberg lives in Chester, Massachusetts.

John Brockman is the author of several works of contemporary philosophy. His books, *By the Late John Brockman, 37,* and *Afterwords,* are the subject of a collection of essays, *After Brockman.* Mr. Brockman is the editor of *Real Time 1, Real Time 2,* and *About Bateson: Essays on Gregory Bateson.* He lives in New York City.

Edwin Schlossberg and John Brockman are the coauthors of *The Pocket Calculator Game Book, The Philosopher's Game,* and *The Pocket Calculator Game Book #2.*